# SURPRISED BY THE SPIRIT

by

## Rev. Edward J. Farrell

DIMENSION BOOKS
Denville, New Jersey

DEDICATED

*To John Cardinal Dearden, to my fellow priests of the Archdiocese of Detroit and to the students of the Sacred Heart Seminary*

*Published by*

DIMENSION BOOKS
Denville, New Jersey

Copyright © 1973 by Edward J. Farrell

# CONTENTS

# FOREWORD:
## PILGRIM OF THE HOLY

Today is Epiphany, 1972. And I am on Cat Island in the Bahamas, continuing a pilgrimage which began decades ago, perhaps far back in the memories of my forebears in Ireland. The story of the Wise Men following a star was woven deeply into my imagination; and last evening as I looked into the sharp clarity of the sky with its glowing southern cross, I felt I might be one of those journeying seekers. Long had I felt the gentle tug and call to go to the Holy Wells, the holy places, the holy people.

There is something of Diogenes in each of us; not so much wanderers with candle in hand searching for the truth but, rather, walkers in the darkness with candles to be lighted. We search for a spark, a light, a flame; for a master teacher to call us forth. What is it I seek? Perhaps in the very search a man becomes what he seeks. Whatever it may mean, this continuing pilgrimage to seek out holy places, holy men, I do know that the Celtic wanderlust was stirred deeply within me in my childhood. Irish feet seem to have an itch which no walking cures. The heart is always ready for the open road, the ear hears and responds to the call to pilgrimage.

Rome, Ireland, Jerusalem, Nazareth, Japan, Nepal, India, Russia, the Sahara — where I was graced with a deep and holy experience — in all these places, and in many others, I have been a pilgrim. Now, through a sister in the Dominican Cloister in Connecticut, who told me of a hermit on Cat Island, and through the Bishop of the Bahamas, I had received an invitation from Father Paré, a Benedictine monk from Martinique. Brother John, as he is known on the Island, had made arrangements for the Scarboro missionaries on the Island to provide for my accommodation and hospitality. Cat Island is in the Bahama chain 300 miles east of the tip of Florida. Until recently it was thought to be San Salvador, the island where Columbus first touched shore. Actually San Salvador is the next island, thirty miles to the southeast.

A Scarboro Father met me at the plane and drove me to the Holy Redeemer parish in New Bright. As we entered the drive, I noticed a bearded workman on the roof of the old convent. It was Brother John himself. Down he came to welcome me as a brother, with a wide smile and unforgettable warm brown eyes with quiet twinkle and silent depths.

As we talked together in the mid-afternoon shade, our backs against the wall of the building he was repairing, it was as if we had always known one another. Very simply he told me of his life. We were both the same age, both ordained on December

16th, although his ordination was ten years later than mine. For almost twenty years he has been a hermit.

A New Englander, Brother John was born and grew up near Boston. He joined a religious community and studied in Montreal, Canada. During his novitiate, he read *The Hermit of Cat Island,* the life of Fra Jerome Hawes (1876-1956), a book which made a lasting impression on his mind. Jerome Hawes, a London-born architect, had served as an Anglican minister and missionary in the Bahamas from 1908-1911. He had been drawn to the Catholic faith and was received into the Church at Graymoor, New York, in 1911. After his ordination in Rome, he went to the missionary fields of Australia where he worked zealously and fruitfully for twenty-five years. There he distinguished himself as a church architect, was made a Monsignor. Yet he had not forgotten the Franciscan ideals which had burned in him in his early years. A desire for poverty began to haunt him; and at last, in 1938, at the age of sixty-two, he made his decision. He would go to the remote Bahamas and become a hermit. He wrote to his Bishop:

> When God calls us (speaking of the Holy Spirit in our conscience) to do certain things we must do them or deteriorate in our spiritual life. I admire the life around me, but there is an inward movement planted by God in my soul, so I believe — an inescapable impulse which for so long, and

for whatever I may do against it, has been forcing me in another direction. I know not, nor does it matter whether God is calling me now for any more work to do, or any sphere of usefulness — it may be only to uproot me for the good of my soul. Even though I may now be useless as a missionary in the Bahamas, I can, amidst the poverty and simplicity of the people on the out islands, live a real Franciscan life in the strict and holy poverty according to the Gospels; which would be impossible to do in Western Australia in anything of the same literal way.

Monsignor Hawes selected Cat Island for its isolation and for its miniature mountain over four hundred feet high, the highest point in the Bahamas. He named it Mount Alverina. There he built the hermitage and the chapel of the Holy Spirit. He did not find the solitude he had hoped for since he was drawn from it to give architectural services and other kinds of help to the surrounding islands. Nor did he escape curiosity seekers. To the end of his life he was in conflict between what he desired and what he was unable to achieve. It seemed that only when he was laid to rest there that he finally came to know that which he had long desired, the peace and solitude of God. He died in 1956 and his body is buried in the little cave on Mount Alverina a few feet from the hermitage he had built. The hermit of Cat Island who had struggled in vain, it seemed, to be a hermit, to be alone, finally had achieved aloneness.

Although it seemed that the usefulness of the hermitage had been ended, and that his call had been a call to him alone, this was not to prove true. For, following in his footsteps not many years later, was Father Lionel Paré who, as was noted, had remembered, treasured in his heart the account written by Monsignor Hawes. In his turn he felt the call to become the hermit. Truly the Spirit blows wherever it pleases. One hears its sounds but cannot tell from whence it comes or whither it goes. That is how it is with all who are born of the Spirit. From Boston to Montreal, to Martinique, to Europe, to British Columbia and to Cat Island, Father Paré would journey, would become a hermit and would live by a rule drawn up by Jacques Winandy, his spiritual father.

Though the hermit life seems to us especially strange today, Pope Paul VI did not hesitate to declare that hermits have truly a pastoral ministry in the church, and this resides in their hidden life itself. The primary role of the minister, of the priest, is to bear witness by his works, to lead by example. The role of hermits is to witness to the prophetic gift, to be the appointed witnesses of the Spirit. How would they not deserve this title, seeing that their very existence would make no sense were it not a sign of the permanence of the Divine, the affirmation of a presence always active, of an ultimate and omega point of which ordinary values offer only a hint. Living for God alone, reducing their needs to the minimum, having no other desire than for heaven, the hermit recalls to the church, always tempted to forget it, that our ultimate purpose is not the building of the city of man but the love and the worship of God. He reminds us by his presence alone that we are on our way to Mount Zion, the City of the Living God, the heavenly Jerusalem, and that we have no right to stop or to look back. Still less have we the right to settle down in comfort.

As I read Brother John's simple rule of the hermits, only a few pages in length, I jotted down several thoughts which impressed me:

— The hermit lives his life cut off from all society, even from those who share with him the search for God.

— The company of men is a distraction from our aim which is purely to seek God.

— Celibacy is the normal state of anyone who wishes to give himself completely to God . . . It is pointless to live without a wife unless we have entered by grace and faith the life of the inner man and have Christ dwelling in our heart.

*Poverty and Work:*

— A great simplicity of life, a reduction of needs to the minimum, a rejection of everything superfluous.

— Aspire to live quietly, to mind your own affairs, to work with your own hands.

*Asceticism of the Body:*

"I treat my body hard and make it obey me, lest after preaching to others, I myself should be disqualified" (I Co. 9:26).

— The three great means: fasting, abstinence and night vigils. "At midnight I rise to praise you" (Psalm 119:62).

I spent many hours with Brother John in conversation and in silence and came to realize anew the truth that the closer one is to God the more deeply human one becomes. One of the first requests I made of John after we had become acquainted was to ask for a word, a blessing of his wisdom, some gift from his prayer, a share in his experience. His response to my request was a deep smile.

During my stay I wrote down many of John's passing remarks. When I asked him about his prayer he said that his prayer has become more and more quiet with fewer and fewer words needed. When he spoke of holiness he observed that "God always covers up His holy ones; they are always eccentric." When St. Therese died her community was wondering, "What can we say about her?"

There was a warm compassion in John for everyone and everything. He mentioned that we learn humility through our sins and once forgiven even our past sins can be a help to us. John explained that spiritual direction is for humility and without humility there is nothing. One has to be mature enough to know he is immature and in need of direction. Father Winandy continues to be his spiritual director through correspondence.

Whatever John did he did with a sort of dancing joy, whether mixing cement for the roof or washing the dishes after supper. We celebrated liturgy together and shared our response to the readings: "Suffering is the indelible mark of the Christian. Suffering happens only because you love." I remember his quoting Augustine, "God is not just. We sin and His Son dies for us." And once he mentioned that people were converted by the Curé of Ars just by looking at him.

After John and I had spent three days together he invited me to spend a few days in solitude in his hermitage. He, no doubt, needed a rest from me and I, too, was anxious to spend more time alone. The hermitage is the most picturesque of holy places; even the richest of imaginations could not dream of it. It stands on the hilltop commanding the whole southern end of Cat Island and is visible from every point of the island. The journey there is a slow two miles through brush and tropical growth and the steep, narrow, winding path prohibits any car or bicycle from approaching it. Fra Jerome had carved striking Stations of the Cross into the coral rock which one passes in the ascent, and they were well placed providing fourteen points of rest on the way up. When we finally reached the summit I was amazed to see the hermitage at close range, for what had appeared at a distance to be able to accommodate a good-sized community I now found was perfectly scaled for one person. The buildings had been so well scaled to their environment that from the shore they appeared ten times larger than they actually were. The chapel is the largest building, five feet wide, eight feet deep and six feet high! To the right of the chapel and to the rear is an exquisite Celtic bell tower, eighteen feet high, where one can sit in the shade the whole day and watch the sun pass over the island. To the left on a crescent is a small study, the kitchen and fireplace; connected by a roofed portico is the hermit's sleeping cell. Bits and corners of the churches Fra Jerome had loved best had found their way into his dwelling. The influence of the primitive Franciscan hermitages in Umbria and Tuscany was evident in the whole layout of the building and the way it appeared to have grown out of the natural rock rather than having been built upon it.

I came to know Fra Jerome better than I had learned to know him through his book. I found it easy to pray beside his tomb for his presence and his spirit had somehow been deposited in these buildings and in the places which he had chosen for his prayer.

There is a strength and power and vision which he breathed into what his hands had created, and the cumulative force of his presence made it easy for me to pray with him and come deeply to admire and love this old hermit.

It is true that place does not create prayer, but it is not difficult to understand why even Our Lord went out to the desert, up to the mountain and even along the lakeside to pray; why He took His disciples to Caesarea Philippi, to Mount Tabor and the Mount of Olives. There is a presence of God which can be experienced only in silence and solitude. The grandeur of nature will continue to speak, however softly, her revelation of the Creator. "The very stones will cry out." I spent three days in solitude on the top of the mountain in the hermit's cell. The more there is to an experience like this, the less there is to say about it. One feels almost foolish in trying to put it into words. What does one dare to say of the dawn?

One of Cat Island's gifts to me was the coolness and stillness of the early morning as I waited, longing for something more than sunrise, watching a new day of my life rise out of the Atlantic. So rarely do we have time to *be,* to listen for the sheer joy of hearing, to feel the early morning. There is so little time that when we do take it to allow what is real to be real to us, it has almost an unreality. Each day God imprints on us and within us a touch of the infinite, a longing for life, a yearning for unending love; we know Him as hidden and distant yet visible and near. He calls us from one degree of awareness to another, from one sense of being possessed to another realization of it. I am aware of having a life lived within me which is beyond my reach but very present to me. Sometimes everything that is outward brings back thoughts of Him to me. Yet it is impossible to rest or reflect at that level or at that moment on these things because they are only reminders to me that He is not met in these things but in the life which is lived within me.

The days went with incredible swiftness, perhaps even more because I tried to hold on to every moment. As I celebrated Mass I could look through the small transparent windows behind the altar and see the light touch the waves. In the evening, the sun set in the direction of the Caribbean and I found myself drawn into the prayer which evening chants. When the sun disappeared, all the sounds of the island were amplified. The beauty of the night was so intense that I lost track of time. It was good to be in prayer and to know that He prayed with me, to follow His footsteps into moments that will never disappear from human history because they are ever continued in His risen life with us. I felt myself one with all those who do not sleep at night – the sick, the dying, the troubled, the despairing; mothers nursing their children, hospital

attendants, police and firemen, mainten-
ance and custodial people; night travelers,
truckers, pilots and sailors, contemplatives.
I felt one with the Eucharist now being
celebrated on the other side of the world,
the Presence that is ever near. He never
sleeps, He is always watching over us and
waiting for us. It was good to keep Him
company, to be present, to wait out the
night with Him.

John came to repossess his hermitage
the third day. We celebrated Eucharist
together quietly. When we had finished our
thanksgiving John turned to me and said,
"When you go back and talk with your
people tell them *to be patient with God, to
wait for Him."* I had forgotten that I had
asked John for "a word." When I had
forgotten, it was given to me. And as I
folded my vestments a deep unforgettable
joy leaped within me and it is still there.

\*　　　\*　　　\*

It has been a year since I left the Cat
Island hermitage and my friend John but
they are very much alive in me and
growing. Brother John in his hermitage
calls me to prayer when I might not
otherwise go. John made real to me some
of those mysterious lines in Leon Bloy's
*Woman Who Was Poor.* "One does not
enter Paradise tomorrow or the next day or
in ten years' time, but 'this day' if one is
poor and crucified. . . . Woman only exists,

in the truest sense, if she is without food, without shelter, without friends, without husband, without children; only thus can she compel her Savior to come down."

The hermit reminds me of the ancient tradition of the Lamed-Vov which is traced back to the time of the prophet Isaiah and the Ebed Yahweh. According to it, the world's continued existence rests upon thirty-six just men, the Lamed-Vov, undistinguished from simple mortals; often they are unaware of their role. But if just one of them were lacking, the sufferings of mankind would poison even the souls of the newborn, and humanity would suffocate with a single cry. For the Lamed-Vov are the hearts of the world multiplied and into them, as into one receptacle, pour all our griefs. "O companions of our ancient exile, as the rivers go to the sea all our tears flow in the heart of God."

It is significant that the hermitage stands in view of San Salvador where, with Columbus' discovery, the modern Americas began. In front of Cat Island runs the Atlantic missile range which has served as a primary landing area for the United States manned space program. As the Apollo flights have continued Columbus' voyage, there is an ever greater need for men to rediscover the Holy Wells and keep them uncovered. Without men who make the spaceless journey to the Center of the universe, civilization will fade into the twilight.

To me it was given to enter into the experience of two men in their "hidden-ness," Fra Jerome and Brother John. In the solitude and silence which they had created I was privileged to spend days in prayer and contemplative quiet. The hermit who lives in all of us cries out for the hermitage, for periods of aloneness with oneself, with God, and I am deeply conscious of the grace given me during my days there.

It is out of the experience of Cat Island, of the Sahara Desert and of other solitudes; out of the retreats I have given during the past year; and from searching the scriptures in which is to be found eternal life, that this book has come into being.

The gifts of the Spirit and the Beat-itudes through which Jesus is revealed draw one ever more deeply into prayer. It is my hope and my prayer that my reflections may speak to the hearts of others who are on pilgrimage to the City of God.

# I  ADORATION AND ABANDONMENT

*"I, the Lord, am your God." "Be still and know that I am God." "From the cloud there came a voice which said, 'This is my Son, the Beloved . . . . Listen to Him.' When the disciples heard this, they fell on their faces, overcome with fear." "They left all and followed Him."*

These sayings suggest an experience of both adoration and abandonment, a total giving, worship, an acknowledgement of the glory of God before which man can only bow in awe and adoration. "Adoration" for the man of today is difficult. He is not altogether sure of what it is, what it means. Yet "adoration" is one of the great continuing words of the religious vocabulary, a vocabulary which is one of the richest, most retentive elements of our language. Words linger on long after the deep experience which they signified has been forgotten. Sometimes, even the capacity for the experience has become dimmed or lost, the meaning of the word blurred. We "adore" many things — the word is in common use, is used to describe lesser and often inane things or ideas. Thus "adoration" in its religious and original sense — the bowing down in awe and reverence, tinged with the fear of God — has become largely lost in superficial wonder and feeling.

"Who is the man who trembles before God?" asks Paul Tillich. It is not that man today is arrogant with the *hubris,* the proud insolence of which the ancient Greeks spoke. Rather, it is an indifference, a non-understanding of awe or of adoration. It is outside the range of our religious experience, of our emotional development. Part of this lack is a result of our contemporary history. Man in every day of his experience is so saturated with both wonders and horrors that his senses can barely respond to the newest overwhelming stimulus. Man feels pride in his having conquered nature, overpassed the law of gravity, in his ever-expanding technological knowledge. He bows down to his own power, yet knows not the meaning of adoration. Yet there will always be some men who refuse to be overwhelmed by the current of the times, who do not surrender to the whirlwind of present events and movements. When the outer senses are flooded the inner ones are compelled to become operative or the spiritual life perishes. One may be tempted, like Elijah, to lie down and wish he were dead. "I have had enough. Take my life; I am no better than my ancestors" (I Kings 19:4). Like Israel, we may desire and be given "A sluggish spirit, unseeing eyes and inattentive ears" (Romans 11:8). Like Jeremiah, we can attempt to say, "I will not think about him. I will not speak in his Name any more" (Jeremiah 20:9).

The temptations do not, however, overcome those with spiritual strength. Suddenly there comes "the sound of a gentle breeze, a fire burning in my heart, imprisoned in my bones. The effort to restrain it wearied me; I could not bear it." Elijah hears the voice, "Elijah, what are you doing here? Arise . . . ."

Over the "trackless waste and emptiness" God's Spirit hovers (Genesis 1:1). A light will shine in the darkness over the deep and all the darkness of time and history will not put out "the true Light that enlightens all men."

In his classic book, *Prayer,* Hans Urs von Balthasar gives a crucial insight, an answer to the question Tillich asked, "Yet who is the man who trembles before God?" "One who has never experienced a deep sense of awe before the Being of God," he writes, "not merely before the 'mysteries of existence' and the profundities of the world, is not yet prepared for the contemplation of Jesus Christ. He ought at least to let himself be educated to this sense of fear and terror through the Old Testament; otherwise he is in danger of coming to Christ deaf and blind, seeing in him only an example of human perfection, and contemplating in Him, not God, but man, which is to say, himself. That the absolute Being of God should have decided to present itself in a human life, and should be able to carry out His will should be a perpetual source of wonder to anyone contemplating the life of Jesus, should seem a thing impossible and utterly bewildering. He ought to feel his mind reeling at the idea, feel as if the ground were giving way under his feet, and experience the same 'ecstacy of incomprehension' which seized Christ's contemporaries" (p. 108).

In Mark's gospel we find over and over again this expression of astonishment; at the cure of the paralytic, "They were all astounded and praised God, saying, 'We have never seen anything like this'!'' When the daughter of Jairus was raised to life, he records, "they were overcome with astonishment." His disciples when He walked on the water, "were utterly and completely dumbfounded." I think Mark would be astounded at our "coolness," our inability to be astonished, our ecstacy fatigue. Our minds and our feelings have been "blown" too often for us to feel the trembling and adoration of which both the Old and New Testaments speak.

Much of our poverty of feeling stems from the fact that our "experience" is really second-hand, substitutional, vicarious experience. Percy Walker's novel, *The Moviegoer,* portrayed a young man whose greatest life experience was seeing John Wayne in *The Stagecoach* shoot three Indians as he was falling to the ground. It is tragic that many feel their lives are pallid and insignificant, dwarfed by the cinema screen and the intensity of TV action and violence. When media portray "real life" then "everyday" life demands artificial stimulation and addiction in order to endure it.

The very poverty of our lives accentuates our need of the promise of Jesus, "I have come to bring you life, life more abundant!" Yet "He was in the world that had its being through Him, and the world did not know Him." God is not a second-hand experience; rather, He is the deepest and most personal experience a man can have of himself. How is one to be ready, how be prepared, how be educated, to meet not the impersonal God but the Hound of Heaven? That inexpressible moment when one is no longer addressing *He* but meeting *You?* "If you but knew the gift of God and who He is that speaks to you . . . ." How often our ears are closed, we pass by unseeing.

You, God, my greatest weakness; my greatest temptation; my greatest fear; my greatest love!

Kadosh, Kadosh, Kadosh
Hagios, Hagios, Hagios,
Sanctus, Sanctus, Sanctus
Holy, Holy, Holy.

The Holy is the most intimate and intensely personal and unitive of all experiences; that which integrates most totally, where all superlatives converge, where the sense of the overflowing ultimate Presence and Joy enwraps and draws one into the ecstacy of wordless adoration. In the fulness and *pleroma* of YOU is mirrored the fulness and pleroma of "I."

Friedrich von Hugel has deeply discerned adoration as "the specifically human element in man." Indeed, adoration is the art and stance most constitutive of man's very humanity, "an immediate datum and demand of man's experience of the real." The most fundamental need, duty, honor and happiness of man is . . . adoration. It is the spirituality of the *Gloria:* "We praise You . . . we adore You . . . we give You thanks for your great glory." Adoration is here the human response to glory, is man's consciousness of God making Himself known to man. The *kabod* or glory of God is the glow of His holiness, the radiance of His power and presence. In the superintensity of His Light and Life, truth and grace become incandescent and transparent. The glory of God is entirely present in Jesus, "the splendour of His glory, the figure of His substance, the radiant light of God's glory and the perfect copy of His nature" (Hebrews 1:3). "For God Who commanded the light to shine out of darkness, has shined in our hearts to give the light of the knowledge of the glory of God which is in the face of Christ Jesus." Jesus is the Lord of Glory and from Him it radiates on men, "and we with our unveiled faces reflecting like mirrors the brightness of the Lord, all grow brighter and brighter as we are turned into the image that we reflect; this is the work of the Lord who is Spirit" (II Co. 3:18).

What a magnificent vision! Yet how remote it is from our everyday experience. Paul writes immediately afterwards, "we are only the earthenware jars that hold this treasure, to make it clear that such an overwhelming power comes from God and not from us." How easily we forget even the deepest graces and how honestly Paul could beg for prayers, lest in preaching to others he himself might become a castaway. The command of Christ for constant watching and prayer is never out of season. Our memories are short. The warnings of the Apocalypse are meant to be disturbing.

"I have this complaint to make; you have less love now than you used to." "I know all about you; how you are reputed to be alive and yet are dead. Wake up; revive what little you have left; it is dying fast. So far I have failed to notice anything in the way you live that my God could honestly call perfect; and yet, do you remember how eager you were when you first heard the message? Hold on to that. Repent. If you do not wake up, I shall come to you like a thief, without telling you at what hour to expect me." "I know all about you; how you are neither hot nor cold. I wish you were one or the other, but since you are neither, only lukewarm, I will spit you out of my mouth."

Harsh as these words sound, they are

uttered in love. "I am the one who reproves and disciplines all those I love; so repent in real earnest." "Look, I am standing at the door, knocking. If one of you hears me calling, and opens the door, I will come in to share his meal, side by side with him."

"Repent" is the first recorded word of Christ's public minstry, his first imperative, a command of inexhaustible meaning. "Repent, be born again, become little children, put on the new man, become an altogether new creature." All of these call for a new response each time we hear them. "If only you would listen to him today . . . ." "For everyone who is in Christ, there is a new creation; the old creation is gone, and now the new one is here."

How does one become a little child? How does one continue to be born into an eternal birth? How discover the new in the daily gospel? It is adoration which supplies the link to man's thrust into the future. Adoration is born of the experience of sacramentality, of the sacred inbreaking to the ordinary of life. In every child the sense of the sacred and mysterious is intuitive and direct. "Heaven lies about us in our infancy," wrote Wordsworth. Later experiences, language, and culture dim our capacity, "shades of the prison house" enclose us, erase the memory of what we had known. Much has to be unlearned in order to rediscover wonder, which is the vestibule to adoration.

The beatitudes are the first steps to

adoration, to that Life lived within me which is beyond my reach but very present to me. How humble, how pure one must be to receive the Light. Next to ourselves, our greatest surprise will always be God. "When I think of the greatness of His plan, I fall on my knees before the Father." "At various times in the past and in various ways God has spoken to us and manifested Himself to us even though we did not recognize who stood in our midst." "Before I formed you in the womb I knew you; before you came to birth, I consecrated you" (Jeremiah 1:5). Can this not be spoken of each one of us called into faith? Remember, try to remember, do not forget what I have done for you.

> "Bless the Lord, O my soul,
> Bless His holy name, all that is in me!
> Bless the Lord, my soul,
> and *remember* all His kindnesses.
>> in forgiving all your offences,
>> in curing all your diseases,
>> in redeeming your life from the pit,
>> in crowning you with love and tenderness,
>> in filling your years with prosperity,
>> in renewing your youth like an eagle's"
>> *Psalm 103.*

Remembrance is the door to adoration; one enters in with celebration and thanksgiving. Salvation History is not an abstraction but an autobiography, unique for each one of us. Parallel to the Liturgical year,

each of us should have our personal cele-
brations of the great moments of His living
His mysteries in us. We should record those
unforgettable moments, those experiences
of faith, hope and forgiveness when the
scales dropped from our eyes, when suddenly we *"know* in whom we believe."
Creation is God's inescapable sacrament,
overflowing with intimations of his magnif-
icence. In the silence of every sunrise and
sunset are seen the golden threads which
hold all of reality together, giving continu-
ity and unity to life. Night mirrors the
divine sparks showered upon us. There are
the holy moments which come to us like
rainbows to quiet us as they open the
depths within us. There are, too, the
once-in-a-lifetime moments – walking in
the fog and coming suddenly upon the
ocean; experiencing at night the endless
depths of the Grand Canyon; waking to the
Sahara dawn; the first glimpse of the
Rocky Mountains.

There are the daily moments, the privileged times of prayer in the final moments
of consciousness before falling asleep; the
slow awaking in the predawn quiet of
Spring; the experience of kinship and the
wordless, touchless embrace of love. All of
these moments are both complete in themselves and, at the same time, prelude the
more intimate epiphanies of His presence
which draw us into Adoration. There
comes a moment when one knows in deep
anguish the infinite distance between one-

self and God, like a lonely satellite launching into outer space. And there is the other moment when one feels deeply immersed in what could only be called the womb of the Father, so total and peace-filling is the experience.

Adoration of God is a long slow life process of interpenetrating manifestation and discovery, a cumulative exploration experience toward an ever-expanding horizon. Each of us is a pilgrim of the Absolute on an immense and limitless journey.

It is only because God is with us that we can find Him. "No one has ever seen God; it is the only Son who is nearest to the Father's heart who has made Him known." "No one can come to the Father except through me." Adoration is a gift: yet God is apprehended only if there be action and response on our part. It demands time and patience, patience with ourselves, a waiting for God. It is not a moment, but a cumulative process. Each day we must come to Him, and wait, allowing Him slowly to deposit His presence in us. Our fidelity to prayer creates a receptiveness in us like that of a photographic plate in the Mt. Palomar telescope. Whether one looks at a distant star field for a minute or all night, the eye senses no more light than in the first wink, for the human eye cannot hold its focus long enough for the distant light to deposit itself. The photographic plate collects light in a cumulative process.

When an astronomer at Mt. Palomar

exposes a photographic plate for ten seconds, it may reveal twenty fairly bright stars. A ten-hour exposure will show 2000 or more stars which are too faint to be seen by the naked eye, even when assisted by the finest of telescopes. So we, when we hear His call, "Come and see," and enter His presence day after day, our prayer makes us like delicate photosensitive plates to God, almost imperceptibly, yet cumulatively collecting His light. Finally we see in the darkness what few others can see; and are able to cry out with Paul, in adoration, "I *know* Him in Whom I have believed."

## II BEATITUDES

### *Blessed Are The Poor*

"Blessed are you."

No stranger words ever startled the ears of the poor, the humble, the meek, the mourning. What had been considered a curse is proclaimed a blessing! A living death is called "a more abundant life." Bad news becomes "Good News."

The beatitudes are Jesus' self-portrait, the most personal description we have of Him in the Gospels. They are the timeless image of Christ. Because the "poor" will be with us always, Jesus will be with us always. The most profound commentary on the Beatitudes is that of the final judgment on us (Matthew 25). The manner in which we have treated the poor, the hungry, the sick, the stranger, reveals our essential view of life. And these words of Jesus give to us an image of Him which we shall have before us all the days of our life.

We have often longed to know what Jesus actually looked like. What would a painting, a photograph have shown us? Would we today recognize Him if we saw Him? Although the mystery of the face of Jesus remains, each of us carries his own inner picture of Him. Consciously or unconsciously we are always looking for the Christ figure Who walks into each of our lives; each of us hopes for a secret or unexpected rendezvous. As an adopted child looks unceasingly for his real parents, or a parent for a missing child hoping for a meeting, a recognition – so we long for the Emmaus experience. "Now as they talked this over, Jesus came and walked by their side, but something prevented them from recognizing Him (Luke 24:15).

We are all, in a sense, Zaccheus, "anxious to see what kind of man Jesus was." Like him we listen to hear our name called as no one has ever spoken it before, to hear him say, "Come down. Hurry, because I must stay at your house today." Yet it is in the Beatitudes that we truly recognize Him. And the Resurrection appearances were a sign of how He would be with us; as a gardener, a stranger, walking on the shore, a service man, knocking on the door; appearing in the blinding light of Paul's conversion.

At the heart of the Beatitudes are the words of Jesus: "I am with you, do not be afraid. I Have called you by name, you are mine. Walk on in peace. Without me you can do nothing; with Me all things are possible." He is with us.

Christ, the Son of God, did not only become man, he became a poor man, became the suffering Servant of Yahweh. "Without beauty, without majesty with no looks to attract our eyes ... a man of

34

sorrows and familiar with suffering . . . he was despised and we took no account of him."

Jesus was poor. Although he could have been otherwise, He chose to be poor. "Foxes have holes, and the birds of the air have nests, but the Son of Man has nowhere to lay his head." Nor did he have anyone on whom to rest his heart. Constantly Paul repeated, "Remember how generous the Lord Jesus was: he was rich, but He became poor for your sake to make you rich out of His poverty." "His state was divine, yet He did not cling to His equality with God but emptied Himself to assume the condition of a slave."

Jesus said, "Blessed are the poor." Yet His poverty is an ever-increasing embarrassment to us today, the words creating an awkward uncomfortableness for priests, religious, and laity alike. "Sell your possessions and give alms." "If you wish to go all the way, go and sell what you own and give the money to the poor." In the Gospels, the poor have an eminent dignity; and real poverty remains a privileged path.

For Jesus, poverty is a kind of sacrament, the value of which can be discerned only from the inside, through living it. To this experience the Gospel invites us, invites us into the heart of Jesus' choosing to be poor — there to discover immense riches. When we invite Him into our hearts, there He will feel our poverty. Because Jesus chooses us He continues to be poor, and if we choose, He takes us, accepts us even in our personal inadequacy. "God chose what is foolish . . . He chose what is weak . . . those who are nothing at all." Poverty is a way of being, of living the reality of truth, of entering into the freedom of Jesus. It is a unique presence to God, creating in us a new relationship to Him, a new attitude to people and things. Once, I remember, a retreat master jolted me by saying, "I am not free to preach the Gospel because I am not poor." A priest friend of mine taught me much about being poor when I heard him again and again invite visitors to take any of his possessions they desired. When I attempted that, the person responded, "What would be most difficult for you to part with?" And then I realized how far I was from being poor.

"Blessed are the poor." It seems, sometimes, that life is one long process of becoming rich, only to become poor. God gives and God takes away. God gave Abraham his Isaac; then asks him to sacrifice him. So, also, His gifts to us become our sacrifice to Him. The true kind of sacrifice which is whole — holy — is when it is freed for God, freed from our possessiveness. As with Abraham's sacrifice, it becomes more ours because it is His. How difficult it is for us to give generously that which we hold most dear. Still more difficult is it for us to leave people free, to love them freely. *My* is a possessive word, and its connotation is divisive unless one becomes poor with the poorness of Christ. Then *my* means, "all that I am is yours."

Each of us can relate a personal litany of poverty:

> I am poor because I am a sinner; poor because I am in need;
> I am poor because of my unconversion, of my unending repetition of failings and weaknesses;
> I am poor because of so little talent, so little energy, so little time.
> I am poor because I need so many people;
> I am poor because time moves faster than my feet, my hands, my mind, and my heart.

When I was a child I could outrun the little brook, leaping back and forth across it. Now life has become an ever-widening stream which outspeeds me, leaving me further and further behind. This experience creates in me a sense of poverty, a renunciation which I must accept.

There is, however, a deeper dimension into which one must enter if he is really to understand poverty. It is in identifying oneself with Jesus' human concern for the poor that one learns the full meaning of poverty. The poverty of another becomes mine. When he becomes poor, I am poor. The confusion within the Church becomes mine. The inarticulate pain of others around the world envelops me. I am poor with the poverty of all men.

Always, however, the Messias of the

poor comforts me because it is for us that He called us to be Church. For the whole of history He continues to be poor in the poverty and powerlessness of His servant; in the Gospel; and in the Sacraments.

Blessed are you who do not possess anyone for you are free to possess and to be possessed by everyone. Blessed and happy are you who are free to be totally Mine. Blessed are you who are Mine for I can give you away. Blessed indeed are the poor!

> Each of us should continue to ask: How has He led me to be poor?
> How does His presence free me to be poor?
> How is poverty a beatitude in my life and what have been its effects upon it?
> How have I led others to discover and to embrace the secret and gift of poverty?

## *Blessed Are The Meek*

The beatitude "Blessed are the Meek," is probably the one most incompatible with our particular culture. Of course, all the beatitudes are really a counterculture. None of them on the human level makes sense. To be meek is certainly to many people a contradiction of the self-affirmation, self-fulfillment and self-development which we have been taught are all-important. It is a virtue difficult to understand.

The Scriptures speak often of meekness. In the New Testament we find: "Learn of Me because I am meek and humble of heart." Humility is an integral part both of poverty and of meekness. "Ours is a gentle Father, the God of all consolation." Meekness is related to gentleness, to kindness, to the mystery of silence, to abandonment and to obedience.

In the first letter of Peter is a powerful statement: "In the inner life of the heart lives the imperishableness of a quiet and gentle spirit, of great price in the sight of the Lord." In the Old Testament, too, are references to this virtue. "Moses was the meekest man on the face of the earth for he was utterly submissive to God." "By waiting and by calm you shall be saved. In quiet and in trust your strength lies." The reward of humble service is Divine intimacy.

What is often not realized is that meekness can be possessed only by a strong person. It is not weakness; rather, I think, it is restrained power. There is beauty in a tremendously powerful person for he can be meek. Moses, because he was powerful, was meek. Meekness, then, is not the mark of the timid, is not the virtue of a weak person. Christ spoke of Himself as being meek and lowly of heart. In Dostoevsky's portrait of the Inquisitor, the full meaning of the power of meekness is shown, a terrifying power. Yet the meek person is one who removes fear from another. Everyone has some fears. There is nothing which frightens us more than other people; attracts us more than other people. In each of us is a fear about what the other person will think or say. But the meek person has capacity to remove this fear. He is a non-threatening person, not out of weakness but out of strength.

Meekness is the capacity to become little, the capacity to suffer a lack of understanding, the capacity to turn a cheek, to love one's enemies, to be able to respond not in violence but in love.

The "Prayer of St. Francis" is one of the most expressive descriptions of what meekness is. It is disciplined love; it is the non-use of our power over others. It is being able to say with John the Baptizer: "He must increase; I must decrease." It is to let our work be done by another, to work ourselves out of a job, to move on, to let go of our position, to train someone to excel us. It is being able to identify with, and to enter into, the life of another person. An Italian movie, "The Miracle of Milan," had as its central character a meek man. This man was able to enter into every person he met. With a blind person he would not use his eyes, with a lame person he would limp. He made a real identification; he was so truly free that he could enter into their lives, truly suffer with them. The true prophet is the meek man, the man who bleeds for the sins of his people.

It is important for us to recognize the gift of meekness that is given to us. For me this gift has become most real through my experience of people, often much older and wiser who have put their trust in me. I think of my first Pastor, Father Mike Collins; his meekness really humbled me. I think of Brother Roger, the Little Brother, and Connie Young, and many others who have put so much trust in me. The gift lies in the beautiful accessibility of great people who are able to make you feel that you are as important as they are.

The word "Islamism" means giving of oneself to God, being ready to serve, ready to give up one's position. Meekness is the counterculture to which Christ calls us. No one really wants the last place; no one scrambles to get it. No one wants the job no one else chooses. No one wants to clean the toilets. I am much impressed by Gandhi's actions. In his lifetime, the only job the untouchables were allowed was to clean the latrines. Gandhi, therefore, no matter where he was would always clean the latrines. Through whatever city he moved, he went always to the untouchable areas so that if any dignitaries wanted to see him they would have to pass through these areas. What a gift of meekness he had!

How difficult it is for a rich man, a popular person, a successful man, a gifted person to enter the kingdom. Yet as Christ said, "With God all things are possible." We are awed by God's meekness with us, by His incredible patience.

In meekness lies the essence of obedience, that virtue upon which Christ centered more than on any other; obedience unto death, obedience to the will of the Father, openness and responsiveness to people. It is a difficult virtue to acquire; difficult but priceless. How do we acquire it ourselves? To what degree are we presenting Christ who is presented not as much by words or ideas but by radiating that particular gift of meekness which draws people past us to Christ?

## *Blessed Are Those Who Mourn, Who Hunger And Thirst For Justice*

A student once told me that his grandmother gave him a suggestion for keeping Lent which had made his Lent the best he had ever had: that he should do a good deed every day that was not in his ordinary routine – a personal act of charity.

The Lenten season is associated in our thought with penance and prayer. What is penitential prayer? Traditionally, penance and prayer have been considered as separate. In both the Old and the New Testaments, the three usual ways of penance were prayer, fasting, and almsgiving. Traditionally, one thought of prayer first as adoration and thanksgiving, then as contrition, and finally as petition. We should consider the relation between penance and prayer. The penitential psalms in the Old Testament remain as some of the most impressive and familiar prayers of the church. We need to discover for ourselves today what kind of prayer is Lenten and what kind of penance is our prayer.

Penance-metanoia - is change, not simply to be free from sin or for change itself, but always in terms of Christ - in terms of identification. Blessed are those who mourn, "Out of the depths I cry to you, O Lord." One of our deepest experiences of God arises from our need to be healed; from the experience of our own sinfulness, of our forgetfulness, of our selfishness. It is out of this cry to God: "Out of the depths . . . ," the depths of our own self-awareness and our own self-knowledge of sin that we cry to be healed. Penance, then, in its fundamental meaning is a cry for forgiveness. It is one of our basic forms of prayer, our prayer for healing and for forgiveness.

This experience, this need of forgiveness for our personal sins is one aspect of penance. But there is also Christ as penitent, not only for my personal sins but in the sense that he took upon himself the sins of all mankind. Consequently, every Christian community and every Christian is committed to the work of redeeming, the work of reparation. The very concept of the passion and death of Christ, the concept of penance in terms of lent, is in the corporal penance and transformation of the entire church; it is not only an individual penance which goes on during the whole year in Lent, it is also a corporate expression of the meaning of the church as Pascal Mystery, co-redeeming and being co-crucified with Christ.

We have a spiritual record of those who identified themselves most with Christ in heroic charity, the victim souls, those making vicarious satisfaction, enduring vicarious suffering. The "victim soul" is the suffering servant who suffers for the sins of others. The IBED YAHWEH theme is the dominant theme throughout the liturgy, even the heart of the Consecration: "the cup of my blood that is shed for the remission of sins." The counterpoint, then, of our personal need of penance, which expands into penance as reparation for the sins of mankind, is the undergoing of conversion. Each one of us is called to a new conversion. Each one of us is called to experience his growing *edge* at this particular point in his life. The coincidence of lent and spring is significant. The very word *lent* is Anglo-Saxon for spring, meaning "new life." It is this new life to which we are called.

In a personal way there is the prayer of suffering, the involuntary suffering which is inherent in our own nature, in the inharmoniousness of the self, of the personality – the lacks, the conflicts within ourselves, the

unresolved personality differentiation between certain parts of ourselves which are
growing and the parts which are not growing. There is the penance also which comes
from life situations and becomes for us an
imperative. There are striking examples of
this kind of penance: St. Monica in her
thirty years of prayer for her son,
Augustine; St. Francis of Assisi in the
experience of the stigmata; Padre Pio in our
own day; Father Solanus in Detroit. This is
the *reality* of the innocent suffering for the
guilty. Often we hear today of some person
who has donated a kidney or an eye for
another person. Sometimes a younger
brother takes the place of an older brother
going into service. There have been cases of
one person substituting for another in
going to prison. This is vicarious suffering,
redemptive.

There is, as is evident, an impressive
number of different life styles of penance.
In the great tradition in the Eastern
Churches, especially the Russian, there is
the way of the pilgrim, the person who
goes during his whole life on pilgrimage;
the hermit, the eremite, the monastic life.
In fact, all religious life is in some way
marked by this voluntary commitment of
oneself and one's life to following in the
footsteps of Christ, overcoming evil by
suffering love even unto death. We see it in
the penance of Mary Magdalene, in the
prophets of the Old Testament, in St.
Paul's life, his suffering in his own flesh

what was lacking in the passion of Christ. Even non-Christian figures like Ghandi who, when there was turmoil or violence among his own people, was a penitent for them. He took it upon himself to fast for his students if they were not responding, not attending or were not growing in the way he thought they should.

In his penance Gandhi showed that he had an understanding of corporate life. He knew that his people could only under-stand what they were doing by seeing its effect upon him, upon someone whom they loved; which is what Christ did – the crucifix. We know this kind of love; it is only by being lifted up that He could draw all men to himself, could teach them to realize the effect of their sin. It seems that in penance-prayer if one is to love with one's whole heart, to have true reverence for another, it sometimes demands violence to oneself. And we so often reverse this truth. We are accustomed to have reverence for ourselves but to act in violence towards others; whereas the violence of penance-prayer is a conversion kind of violence – the dying to oneself in order that some others may live more freely in openness to others.

Dom Marmion has written well of com-punction, what suffering love means; it is the entering into the heart of Christ and knowing what sin really is: the lack of love.

It seems that the more one prays, the more penance enters into one's life. Real prayer turns into some form of penance, some form of a deeper conversion. Penance is unitive and prayer is unitive; the more one realizes the love of Christ and the needs of other people, the more one wants to have burned out of his life that which is hindering the way he wants to love, the way he wants to be free, the way he wants to give. It becomes more and more an identifying with Christ; a letting go of those things which hinder this identification. One finds himself more and more in an on-going state of penance, in a more inclusive conversion, spending himself more totally.

One of the signs that this is genuine penance is joy. Throughout Paul's letters one of his most frequent words is "joy." Everyone must suffer both from oneself and from others, but the mark of whether it is Christian or not is the mark of joy and peace. That is what is redemptive. There can be identical suffering, but suffering as such is not necessarily redemptive. It can be a suffering in despair and resentment; but the seal of Christian suffering, of Christian penance, is joy. This is what Our Lord says at the beginning of Lent, "Don't go around mourning, don't go around with long faces." Often the religious thinks about how difficult life is; how terribly lonely. This is counterfeit.

Not long ago I was talking to my younger sister. Her children had been sick — all four of them were sick one night. She told me the long story and I responded, "Ah, if you think that's tough, you should think of all the loneliness and quiet I have." She said, "I'll trade you." She wanted me to know that I had chosen the better part and I said, "I agree."

There is a nursing sister who is working in the Detroit General Hospital. She is really scarred by the kind of non-care many patients have – merely minimal care. She was crying out that in the face of this suffering how unreal so many things seemed to her. "Where," she asked, "is the reality of Christ and the reality of the church?" She accused me, "You live a comfortable life." This "comfortable life"! I felt embarrassed, and I think rightly so. It is not a bad life. We can always go home at night no matter where we are. There is always a place for us to lay our heads. Again and again we have to be challenged. We become used to too comfortable a style of life; we tend to forget, to become immune to the suffering constantly going on; or we experience our overwhelming incapacity to do much about it. This is perhaps the suffering which we bear about in ourselves, and sometimes it does not seem to be too much. Paul spoke often of the anxiety he felt for the churches -- the concern he had for their well being. I am sure that many times when we seem up-tight it is because of the constant concern we have for particular people whom we know we cannot help. The sense of unmitigated tragedy is part of our life; is a real carrying about within ourselves the reality of the sufferings of Christ. This, too, forms a part of our prayer, of our penance.

Much is in the words "Can you drink the cup that I am to drink?," Christ asked James and John. Their glib answer revealed how much they had yet to learn. Our own sufferings, as we learn more of Christ, touch us less than those of others; most of all because there is nothing we can do but be present with them. Especially do we suffer when they have such a deep belief in us and really ask us to work a miracle for them. At times the miracle that is worked is worked by the person himself. It is not merely a matter of being with him because we cannot *be* with him as someone who has no hope. Often, at least in my own experience of hoping, in hoping enough the person transforms that little seed of hope and gives back to me a hope far greater than I had at the beginning. The word of Christ given to suffering people effects a kind of metamorphosis, a transformation which happens when they in turn give you a courage you did not at first possess. This is a great gift — that some people suffer much, but make of it the kind of suffering which becomes a grace.

It is a tangible kind of grace they minister to others in the extraordinary strength that comes in these critical mo-ments of life. It does not happen frequent-ly, but it happens enough that one has — at least I have found it so — a new capacity to have hope and to have courage in the face of absurd suffering, pointless and meaningless suffering; watching a mother of seven children dying of cancer at the age of thirty-four, bringing Communion to her a couple of times a week, and watching her in the course of six months be reduced to a skeleton. Yet she did not despair, she did not give up although she would have if she had not had that extraordinary kind of grace. There is something that we cannot possibly know when we stand with the suffering, but there is something given to us by the suffering which enables us to give this grace to others who do not have it. It grows out of the beautiful kind of interrelationship through which one receives from one person in order to give to another. They give you the fruit of their suffering so that you can pass it on to someone else. This is, I think, one of the great consolations of the nursing profession. To them this experience comes often enough to enable them to go deeper into it — and into the confessional experience as well. Sometimes the person's suffering is healing; and their capacity to heal is in proportion to their suffering.

I was very much moved by the death in Detroit of the Sister at St. Cecilia convent. Her death by a random bullet from a sniper's gun touched the entire community and her blood is in some way redemptive in the whole archdiocese. I think Sr. Julita

will have a profound and far-reaching effect
upon our Archdiocese. She was only one of
600 murdered in the city last year, and the
other sister who was attacked was probably
only one of a thousand who suffered the
same kind of violence. By the fact they
were in the midst of it, they are numbered
among the innocents who day after day
suffer violence and death. It is deeply
disturbing to realize that in our Christian
community two people will be murdered
today and that other kinds of violence will
occur. This tragic fact must enter into our
prayer, together with all other accidental
deaths. It deepens our corporate sense of
responsibility, making us suffering servants
in a unique way. The Mass becomes even
more central to what our living in Christ
means; it tells us again and again as we go
to the altar.

One night for a few minutes after the
Bible Vigil I stopped in the choir loft and
looked down at our chapel; it was empty.
For some reason, the main altar struck me
— the altar as a tomb. I had a flashback of
being in Moscow and watching the number
of people constantly, at every moment,
passing by Lenin's tomb. There is never a
moment, night or day, that the procession
does not file by to venerate the father of
the country; and at every hour there is a
mass convergence for the changing of the
guard. It is one of the few rituals in Russia.
That continuing devotion impressed me.
And it called me to a new awareness of the

mystery of our going as Christians day after day to celebrate not only the death of Christ but also His presence with us. It is Pascal's description of Christ hanging upon the cross until the end of time. And his body of humanity — the whole meaning of the passion and death of Christ is in these days so easy to forget. St. Bernard always said if you wanted to get to know Christ, study the crucifix, study the cross. That study will reveal who Christ is. The Carmelities have their little saying beneath each crucifix: "And no one thinks of it." The real presence of Christ — the love of Christ, in the midst of all the sin and suffering of the world. How many times Christ dies this day; how many times he rises in the heart of every person. For us there should be the constant entering into the passion and death of Christ. It is good to make the little pilgrimage of the Way of the Cross with someone else and to share our meditations. One of my students mentioned taking his CCD class into church, taking them on pilgrimage around the stations of the cross; then meditating on the Eucharist as the 15th station.

We have been speaking somewhat individually about penance, prayer, entering into the suffering of Christ. There is, however, another and significant aspect of penance which is corporate penance. We still do not know how to celebrate the Sacrament of Penance corporately. One of our great limitations has been the contraction of Eucharist and Penance to simply an I-Thou relationship — the vertical relationship between God and oneself. We do not have the way of actualizing the grace of the Eucharist horizontally and actualizing horizontally the grace of Penance. We end the sacrament when it should be beginning its horizontal outreach to one another. We really seem not to know how to take the grace of the Eucharist which is a deeper communion with one another and in some way to make it visible. For most of us it remains very much interior; and the same is true of the sacrament of Penance; we do not really know how to actualize that grace of being forgiven — to forgive one another — to heal one another.

Penance would seem in one deep aspect of its meaning to suffer day by day, to suffer in peace as Paul did, even in joy, to hold oneself in readiness to become the suffering servant, to follow Christ even to death. For all of us it calls for a daily offering of all we are to God, to pray without ceasing.

## *Blessed Are The Merciful*

The beatitudes have to do with the *anawim;* the poor, the meek, the sorrowful, the mournful, those who hunger and thirst. The last four of them speak to the defenders and protectors of the *anawim* — the merciful, the pure of heart, the peace-makers, and those who suffer persecution.

"Blessed are the Merciful." What is the meaning of mercy? The word *mercy,* like *holy,* applies only to God. We cannot give mercy to God; we can love Him, we can adore, we can believe in Him, hope in Him, but we cannot give Him mercy. This relationship is, in a sense, one-way; from God to us. Any time we know mercy it is because He is in us exercising His mercy. The merciful, therefore, are those who have so deep a union with God that they give forth His mercy. At the heart of it is the desire to save the sinner. To love a person implies that he is worthy of love, whereas to show mercy is to show a unique kind of love, love for someone not really lovable, the sinner. It is God in His Divine tenderness who triumphs over sin without in any way compromising His holiness.

This Divine tenderness is shown in Jeremiah 31:20: "Is Ephraim my precious son; is he my darling child? For as often as I threaten him I must always think of him; therefore, my heart yearns for him; I must have pity upon him." Also, it is implicit in the great story of salvation history. There is the convenant call; the infidelity and sin; the punishment and correction; then the mercy and conversion. God calls, but often man is unfaithful; God must then correct him, showing mercy and leading him to conversion. In the very correction lies His mercy.

Psalm 51, the great psalm of mercy, the Miserere, is the psalm of the uniqueness of mercy and forgiveness. There is no parallel in any other world religion of this concept of sin and mercy, of the distinctive relationship of man to God, to the God of the Old Testament and especially to the God of the New Testament. It is hard to believe in the mercy of another person. Mercy is not natural to man. Yet the very word *father* is a word of mercy. The concept which Christ gave us of *Father* is mercy; it involves tenderness. We find it in the great cry of the liturgy, the Kyrie, Lord Have Mercy. We find it in the letter to Timothy: " ... Christ Jesus came into the world to save sinners. I myself am the greatest of them; and if mercy has been shown to me, it is because Jesus Christ meant to make me the greatest evidence of his inexhaustible patience for all the other people who would later have to trust in him to come to eternal life" (1 Timothy 1:15-17). The central role which mercy must play in our lives is in our call to perfection. What is perfection? "It is to be merciful as your Father is merciful." Throughout the New Testament, the saying of the prophets of the Old Testament is emphasized, "what I want is mercy not sacrifice." This idea is repeated again and again by Christ. "It is not the healthy who need the doctor, but the sick. Go and learn the meaning of the words: *What I want is mercy, not sacrifice.* And indeed I did not come to call the virtuous, but sinners" (Matthew 9:12-13). In Luke's gospel, the special gospel of mercy, we find the parable of the Good Samaritan, and in Matthew the great parable of the unjust debtor in which the penetrating question is asked, "Were you not bound, then, to have mercy on your fellow-servant just as I had mercy on you?" Mercy and forgiveness are in the whole notion of the *Our Father*, "Forgive as you have been forgiven."

In the Sacrament of Penance we learn to give one another the grace of that sacrament. The grace of the Sacrament of Penance is in forgiving one another, not in being forgiven by God. The love of God is found only in those who show mercy. In the first letter of John, he says, "If a man who was rich enough in this world's goods saw that one of his brothers was in need, but closed his heart to him, how could the love of God be living in him?"

"Blessed are the merciful for they shall have mercy shown them." The corporal and spiritual works of mercy, "I was hungry, poor and naked . . . what you did to the least of these my brethren, you did to Me." This is the test finally of our love of God, of our capacity to show mercy.

In the story of Jonah, through the dramatizing of his inability to give mercy, we are shown the contrast between the mercy of God and the smallness of ourselves. "The love of God is broader than the measure of man's mind." Luke records the parables of the lost sheep, the lost coin, the wayward son. Paul in his letter to the Romans makes clear man's duty to accept the weakness of others and to forgive. To forgive is to be willing to suffer from a person until your loving kindness heals him. Hosea illustrates this in his taking Gomer again into his home. He was a merciful man, a prototype of Christ. To become a victim, a suffering servant, allowing someone to hurt you until there is nothing left of the hatred in him; this is mercy and love.

The God of mercy is a constant refrain in the psalms. "Give thanks to the Lord for His love, His mercy is eternal." The whole concept of the salvation of the sinner runs, like a silver thread, through the Scriptures.

Try to reflect on your experience of mercy. How often have we failed to experience another person as being of our own family; how often shown our inability to be truly sister, to be truly brother. "Be you perfect as your Heavenly Father is perfect," which means, in this beatitude, "Be you as merciful, because if you are not, in the degree that you are not, so will He be towards you." We should ask ourselves: Is Jesus exercising His mercy in us? Are we instruments, making the beatitudes live in one another and in the world? Mercy is the powerful attribute of Christ; it is tenderness in action.

## Blessed Are The Pure In Heart

So familiar have we become with the beatitudes that all too often our hearing has become the hearing of the ear, not the total attention of the heart. In simple, one syllable words. Christ, in this beatitude, made an infinitely profound statement concerning the spiritual life. He stated both condition and reward. It is good for us to consider carefully and with reverence what He said, what the words mean to our spiritual growth. Since the Beatitudes are Christ's personal self-portrait, since it is in them we find revealed the deep springs of His life, we must deeply ponder the words he has spoken.

Pure in heart. To have nothing extraneous, no dimming of the illumined flame of a singleness in devotion and loyalty. It is, in the context of Jesus' teaching, a wholeness, a complete and permanent commitment to loving God, to seeking to do His will. "You will seek Me and you will find Me when you seek Me with all your heart." The words suggest a splendor, a compelling vision possessed by the person of the undivided heart:

> "Who seeks the Truth must be content to go alone,
> must know himself with a knowledge none can share,
> must have a faith he bears within himself which is a song within his heart, wings upon his heel."

What seems almost a paradox is that Jesus, the pure of heart, could see through the layers of sin and the general murkiness of human life to call forth the purity unrecognized by others, unrecognized by the individual himself. "Come down, Zaccheus," and from that day, that call, Zaccheus was able to assume his birthright as a son of Abraham. "Did no man condemn you? . . . Neither do I condemn you." The sinner rejoices in a new orientation, changes the direction of his life. Jesus confers on him a new dignity and his life, henceforth, is whole, singlehearted.

Always in the encounters of Jesus with persons, there is a quiet simplicity. No fanfare, no argument. One must believe that it was the shining of His own purity which touched those who were open to His teaching. "He who has ears to hear let him hear," "Take care what you hear" – the warning is a preface to the parables. Again and again, the warning: No man can serve two masters. He who seeks God must leave all double dealings (Wisdom 1:1). Jesus says, in effect, that to follow Him means to lose one's life, to die to all that would deflect from the simplicity of being His disciple. "I do always the will of my Father," He said.

Purity of heart can dwell only with nobility of soul, one which has made a full oblation. In the great dialogue between God and Solomon (1 Kings: 9:4) God requires of Solomon an innocence of heart.

In James' exhortation it is a concern to *be* only for God, only to do His will, the will of God in Christ. "Seek first the kingdom of God and all else will be added." This exclusive intention illuminates one's whole life, giving one the zeal to do God's will with the simplicity of the dove, and the wisdom of the serpent.

Implicit in purity of heart is the hatred of sin. It is not saying, "I don't want to make any enemies. You live your way, and I shall live mine." There is no middle ground for the man of passionate heart.

When the Lord responded to the spontaneous exclamation from a man in the crowd, "Blessed is the womb that bore you," with "Blessed rather are those who hear the word and keep it," He made clear the need of having the receptive heart, longing and waiting. For completion of life one must hear the word, keep the word, and finally, become the word.

Blessed indeed to see the hidden God who infinitely exceeds anything man can imagine. "In your light, we see light." To His disciples Jesus said, "You have been purified because of the word I have spoken to you." Such purity of heart comes especially through the word of God, not only as an intellectual assent of the mind, but as a pervasive acceptance in one's total being. What we receive, we become; we become the very word of God. It is the Eucharistic experience.

The second part of the beatitude com-

pletes and fulfills the first. Happy are the
pure in heart; *They Shall See God.* When
the disciples of Jesus first saw Christ they
asked Him, "Where do you live?" Our Lord
said simply, "Come and see." If we can live
where Jesus lived, in the fulness of love of
the Father, if we can *see,* be open constantly to the word of God, in purity of purpose
enter into it in faith, we shall see God.
Reflect on this amazing promise. To try to
stand before God in the brightness of His
shining, to live in a singleness of devotion,
in an undivided spirit of love and loyalty –
this was how our Lord lived; this is the life
He opened to the kingdom of all believers.
Let us accept His blessing.

### Blessed Are The Peacemakers

The root of the Hebrew word "Shalom"
means being intact, being complete. To
wish one shalom is to wish him intactness,
wholeness. In daily life it translates into
wishing man harmony with himself, with
nature, with God; to have fullness of
happiness.

The Hebrew "Yahweh Shalom" means
the God of peace. The words represent the
Old Testament hope, the hope which came
to fulfillment, found its fruition, in Christ.
He is our peace; through Him we can
become peacemakers.

"Peace" as it is used in the New Testament has a density of meaning. In it is included the basic element of forgiveness. Jesus is the man of peace, bringing to us that peace which arises from the love and forgiveness with which he fills our restless hearts. The sign of His peace is His love and joy which we experience in our lives.

The prayer of St. Francis, "Make me an instrument of your peace . . . where there is hatred, let me sow love . . .," shows clearly this close relationship between peace and forgiveness. Where anger dwells there can be no peace. Nor is a superficial "forgiveness," which costs little, peace-bringing. Rather, peace is the *pleroma,* the fullness of the Holy Spirit through which we forgive and are forgiven, know the peace of Christ.

From the annunciation story, "Peace on earth to men of good will," to the Resurrection, "Peace be with you," we are called to be in peace and to make peace. This underscores another aspect of the beatitude; that of fraternity – community. One cannot have peace all by oneself – it arises from relationship with others.

When Jesus sent his disciples on their first evangelical work He told them to say as they entered a town, "Peace to this house and to this town." If the peace were not accepted, if they were not joyfully received, they were to leave; were, in a sense, to recall the offered peace. The people of that town would remain unreconciled, unaware of the peace of Christ whose emissaries the disciples were.

Shortly before His crucifixion Jesus, looking from the hill over Jerusalem, wept because of the refusal of its people to receive Him. "If you had only understood this day the message of peace," He grieved. He knew, and was saddened by the knowledge, that disorder and destruction would follow their rejection – or lack of recognition – of the opportunity God had offered.

What was true of Jerusalem is undoubtedly true of our individual lives. Lacking the inner peace which comes from being in Christ, we are without serenity. When we seek not the things of God, we are bedevilled by confusion and by the conflicting forces within our own nature. Far from being peacemakers we are disorder creators. We are not sons of God if we choose to serve another master. It is a sobering thought; for the choice is before us, the conditions are clear – and we, in our pride, so often choose the destructive path. To be a peacemaker for others, we must first make peace within ourselves, become receivers of the peace of Christ. When we glibly say "Peace be with you" during Mass it should not be a mere formula of empty words but a prayer from the depth of our being. We are called to be in peace and to make peace, to give it to others.

To possess Christ's peace is to be freed from fear. The evangelist Luke is the one who speaks most often of peace. And in his gospel we discover another emphasis of peace; "Do not be afraid," or literally, "I forbid you to be afraid." The story of Christ's quelling the tumult of the waters is symbolic of His calming our fears. "Peace, it is I, be not afraid," or "Why are you fearful, you of little faith." It is a recurrent, reassuring word, "Be at peace, fear not."

In a broader context are the words of Vatican II, *gaudiam et spes,* joy and hope. They represent the overflow of peace, and are the message of the Church to the contemporary world. Although conflict is everywhere present, we have Christ's word: "I have overcome the world." The Church is His sign, must fulfill His purpose, be an instrument of His peace in a world torn by strife and the brutality of war.

A basic role of the Church is to bring reconciliation with God. The great gift of the Father to Jesus was the peace which means the union of man with God in Christ. This is the word Jesus speaks when He says to His disciples, *"My peace* I leave with you." The disciples were to know fear, experience persecution and violence — yet Jesus had given to them His own peace, the enabling power to endure. Repeatedly, Paul underlines this thought. He begins every letter with "Grace and peace." Grace is the effect of Christ's presence in us. He has established us in His peace, even in trial and testing. The fruit of the Spirit is the peace which surpasses all understanding. In his gospel, John describes peace quite simply as the presence of Jesus who established peace through his victory over death. "To as many as believed He gave them the power to become the sons of God," sons of God in the only Son, Jesus.

There is yet another element contained in the density of meaning in this beatitude. It lies in Jesus' statement, "I have come not to bring peace but a sword." His own life demonstrated this truth. A man of peace, he yet created controversy and division, sharply dividing every group. What was true of His life, was true in Paul's experience, in that of his disciples, and of the Church. It is one of the strange paradoxes of the faith and will always be so. It will be a sign of division, a contradiction. It will bring division even in families; it will break natural bonds. The peace of Christ, the kingdom, comes, strangely enough, only by violence; and only those with courage and faith are able to achieve this peace. As long as sin is not dead in man, peace is not a reality; yet the peace of Christ is ever present, will continue to be until the *eschaton.* For Christ is with us, and He is our peace.

Christ alone can establish the definitive and universal peace. Man of himself cannot do it. The Church, the Body of Christ, is the sign and source on earth of peace among people and the giver of the Spirit; it cannot be separated from the reality of Christ. Ultimately, only justice before God and among men can be the foundation of peace, and to achieve this justice the Church must address itself.

The beatitude thus reveals that no one can be an instrument in spreading God's peace unless he, himself, lives in Christ. He then becomes a peacemaker. It reveals, also, that being a peacemaker is a corporate reality. In the dimension of Christ's teaching it is not merely a matter of having peace but also of making peace. And to be peacemakers may cause estrangement and suffering.

Never has it been more necessary than it is today for the individual and for the Church to create peace. In a world of fear and hostility, we are required to learn of Christ, to gain the necessary artistry and skill of peacemaking. We are called to know deeply the blessedness of living in the peace of Christ, to be "reconciler," to heal, as far as we are able, the hurt of the world. Then shall we experience the beauty of being the children of God.

### Blessed Are Those Who Are Persecuted

"Blessed are those who are persecuted" in the cause of goodness, for Christ's sake. The fulfillment of this beatitude lies in becoming a witness to Christ. Throughout the gospel emphasis is on this witness and on the persecution which will be its inevitable accompaniment. "The disciple cannot be greater than his master," nor can he expect different treatment. "If they have persecuted me, they will persecute you."

A wide difference exists between being persecuted and being paranoid. There is a difference also between persecution and suffering. Suffering is universal; whoever he may be no man can escape it, whether he believes, whether he does not believe; whereas persecution is distinctive, individual. It is distinctive in its origin. One may be persecuted because he is just, because he does not conform, because he is faithful. Many people feel they are persecuted or misunderstood and one must be discerning to be sure that it is persecution because he is just, is faithful, is true; not because he is confused.

The mystery which underlies persecution is the evil spirit. There is no way of accounting for it except as the work of the evil spirit, Satan himself and his effort to initiate and to foster the evil which grows in man's heart. We need, therefore, constancy and faithfulness under persecution because it is a test; it is a temptation which calls for prudence. At times this prudence dictates that we should escape. Our Lord knew when He should leave a town or a village and be on His way. His time had not yet come to die. Ultimately, persecution is truly authentic and significant when it arises from one's love of God and fidelity to His word. A kind of persecution may indeed come because one is hard to get along with, or because one is non-

conforming, or different, but the persecution for righteousness' sake is the result of
loving God and being faithful to Him.

*Wisdom,* one of the latest books of the
Old Testament, sums up the profound
motive of all persecution, "The godless
hate the just because he is for him a living
reproach while he is at the same time a
witness to God whom he despises." The
ultimate reason why Christ was removed
was because he was an indictment of the
pharisee, he was an indictment of all their
false values. Those who are persecuted for
righteousness' sake are persecuted because
they also are a reproach, an indictment, a
witness to the God whom their persecutors
despise or fear.

Once Christ harshly called the pharisees
sons of satan because they were like their
fathers who had killed the prophets. Each
time He mentions his coming Passion and
death Christ reminds his disciples that if
they follow Him, they will undergo the
same suffering. They must drink his cup
and be baptized with his baptism.

The lives of the prophets of the Old
Testament ended in persecution and ultimately in death. Jeremiah's life and death
provide a classic example; Isaiah describes
in unforgettable words the suffering servant
of Yahweh; and in the letter to the
Hebrews is a vivid account of all that the
men of vision in both Old Testament times
and New endured. Truly, fidelity to God
leads inevitably to persecution — "You

must drink of the cup that I drink." "You will be imprisoned, beaten, put to death." The story of Paul's suffering merits frequent meditation on the persecution which integrity of discipleship involves.

Although this suffering is inevitable, it provides, nonetheless, a deep source of joy. In the midst of the refrain, "you will be beaten, imprisoned, put to death," another note is sounded. Christ's cry of triumph, "Do not be afraid. I have overcome the world," transmutes the suffering to joy and peace, gives courage. It is the hope, the trust, which makes possible the transcendence of fear. "Do not fear," Christ told his disciples; "when they take you before the courts the Holy Spirit will give you the words to speak." He knew that "the spirit is willing but the flesh is weak." No one seeks martyrdom. We do not wholeheartedly take it on unless we are called to it. *A Man for All Seasons* strikingly expressed the reality of undergoing death for one's faith. It was not the choice Thomas More would have made and, to the last moment, he rebelled against having to face a martyr's death. No naive idealism here, but utter realization of the meaning of fidelity. Jesus, persecuted and alone, cries "Let this cup pass," but follows it immediately with, "Your will, not mine."

Thus every disciple faces persecution, and is enabled to do so because he knows "in whom he has placed his trust." In all his tribulations, Paul experiences joy abounding, a consolation which is a fruit of the Spirit.

In a wider context the book of the Apocalypse speaks of the Church in persecution, of the blood of the saints poured out. The Church will continue in this kind of siege to the end of time. Yet there also is the note of hope: "Do not be afraid of the suffering which awaits you."

In our own day, the Christian must face difficult, often unrecognized, persecution. It is the psychic persecution, the cultural conditioning, the counterculture which so subtly becomes part of ourselves. We need a very special grace of the Spirit to help us discern what is influencing and conditioning us. Sometimes we confuse cultural values and the so-called new values, thereby denying the values of the gospel. There is spiritual deprivation, the deprivation of silence and of time, the over-stimulation of the senses, the verbal saturation, the temptation. We seem to have a knack for being always ready for the wrong attack in the wrong place. So easily like sheep we are led astray, so easily seduced, so easily become an occupied country without being aware of it. So often we surrender parts of ourselves without ever realizing that we have turned a decisive corner in our life.

Temptation is not always recognized or discerned as persecution. Yet it is the satanic persecution of those who would be righteous, those who desire to know God's design for their lives. The temptations of

Thomas à Becket described in Eliot's *Murder in the Cathedral* were, in reality, persecution. Such temptations were not so much in the personal struggle for perfection, although that was an element in it, as in the context of accomplishing God's design.

If we are seriously involved in living the Christian life, we have each to ask, "What is God's will for me?" How do we distinguish between what is our personal fulfillment and what may be a strange call from God cutting across the use of our own particular talents? The line of self-fulfillment is not necessarily the line God asks us to follow. We are confronted by a choice: a choice between the "human" way, and the way God offers in the new design. To take the way God offers will undoubtedly lead to persecution — and to blessedness.

One may be called to be the saint he does not want to become; or to work in ways contrary to his own plans; to suffer persecution through speaking God's word. Moses, Amos, Isaiah; all were called to fare forth on difficult paths. All were tempted to refuse. All suffered persecution.

The temptations of Christ revealed the power of evil in action, the satanic persecution. To refuse or to accept redemptive suffering; to experience the desert; the temptation to become the earthly messiah; the decision to choose God's gift of blessing, fulfilling the beatitude. Can one ever comprehend the depth and terror of that struggle? Yet in the end, Christ said: Blessed are those who are persecuted for righteousness' sake.

Not only does there come to us the primary call. There is also the continuous call. Again and again we must choose God, walk further than we had ever imagined. This is the second vocation, the second calling. It is the point in our life when, as it was in the life of the Lord's disciples, He calls us not to a different vocation but to a new depth and height. It is a calling to live and to die in a way which we had never dreamed would be asked of us.

In this new stage, the second spiral, we discover our deeper vocation. We must then make a decision. What will we settle for, choose? Will we settle for getting by, or for becoming radical in our vocation; settle for the values of our environment, or for deeply living the values of Christ?

If we are overcome by what Nouwen calls the double polarity, the attraction we feel not only to light, but also at the same time to darkness; if we fail to discern the ever-increasing subtlety of our own self-will, we shall not choose to live more deeply. Nor shall we know in any full measure the meaning of the blessedness Christ promised.

Blessed are you when people abuse you and persecute you and speak all kinds of calumny against you on my account. Rejoice and be glad. Happy those who are persecuted in the cause of right. Theirs is the kingdom of heaven.

## III THE GIFTS OF THE HOLY SPIRIT

"All life, all holiness comes from You through Your Son, Jesus Christ our Lord, by the *working* of the Holy Spirit" (Eucharistic Prayer III). "We have received the Spirit that comes from God to teach us to understand the gifts that He has given us" (I Co. 2:12).

As his first gift to those who believe, to complete his work on earth and bring us the fullness of grace. (Eucharistic Prayer IV)

"On Him the Spirit of Yahweh rests,
a spirit of wisdom and understanding,
a spirit of counsel and courage,
a spirit of knowledge and the fear of Yahweh" (Isaiah 11:2).

The *mandala* of the Holy Spirit is multi-splendored, and no prism of word or symbol can capture the manifold expression or the poly-dimensional reality of His presence and work. The Christian Community has long meditated on the utterance of Isaiah that the Messiah would be clothed with the special gifts of his great predecessors: the wisdom and understanding of Solomon, the heroism and prudence of David, the knowledge and fear of God — characteristic of patriarch and prophet, of Moses, of Jacob, of Abraham. The Greek text of the Hebrew Scriptures added the virtue "piety," a repetition of the Hebrew "fear of Yahweh." This seventh gift of piety is, no doubt, symbolic of the fullness and perfection of the Spirit, the countless pleroma of gifts which "if all were written down, the world itself, I suppose, would not hold all the books that would have to be written" (John 21:25).

The promises Jesus made concerning the gifts of the Holy Spirit fill us with awe. "Greater things than I have done, you will do," and "Not many days from now you will be baptized with the Holy Spirit" (Acts 1:5). "You will receive power when the Holy Spirit comes on you, and you will be my witnesses" (Acts 1:8).

The Holy Spirit who brooded over the waters (Genesis); who "overshadowed" Mary in the Incarnation; who made His presence felt at Pentecost when the disciples were "filled with the Holy Spirit" (Acts 2:4) is the same Holy Spirit who continues to be "so lavishly poured over us" (Titus 3:6). "If the Spirit of Him who raised Jesus from the dead is living in you, then He who raised Jesus from the dead will give life to your mortal bodies through his Spirit living in you" (Romans 8:11).

One is "filled with amazement" by the works of the Holy Spirit: Creation, Incarnation, Resurrection, Pentecost. And now at work in us! The Comforter. Although the world is seamed by man's misuse of it: —

> "Generations have trod, have trod, have trod;
> And all is seared with trade; bleared, smear-ed with toil;
> and wears man's smudge and shares man's smell; the soil
> Is bare now, nor can foot feel, being shod."

Nevertheless,

> "And for all this, nature is never spent;
> There lives the dearest freshness deep down things;
> And though the last lights off the black West went
> Oh, morning, at the brown brink eastward, springs —
> Because the Holy Ghost over the bent
> World broods with warm breast and with ah! bright wings."
>
> *(Gerard Manley Hopkins)*

The world is still God's world. Christ has loved us and called us. The work He has begun the Spirit will bring to completion. He has breathed His Spirit into us, gifted us with new capacities and new intuitions. Taught by the Spirit, we can discern the things of the Spirit. Through the gifts given us we are equipped with inner radar and gyroscope, spiritual navigational tools. If we use the gifts well, we shall grow, they will develop. They are buds to be carefully tended; not all will develop at the same time and rate, for each gift has its season, its special moment in the life of the Spirit when it will come to fulfillment.

Christ tells us why He has come – that we may "have life and have it to the full" (John 10:10). He tells us that it is eternal life to know Him and the only true God who sent Him into the world (John 15:3). To what an immense stretching of mind and heart we are called, to an ever-developing consciousness and understanding so that He may share more of himself with us. Not content merely with loving us, He wants us to know Who it is who loves us that we may be able to love Him in return with the same kind of love. He does not wish us to remain as little children, but to grow into the full stature of Christ himself. As Paul says, "in this way we are all to come to unity in our faith and in our knowledge of the Son of God, until we become the perfect man, fully mature with the fullness of Christ himself. Then we shall not be children any longer" (Ephesians 4:13). So He continues to pour into us His Spirit "to teach us to understand the gifts He has given us" (1 Co. 2:12).

Each of us is called to discern the Spirit's work, to recognize the ongoing history of His gifts in us. They are not to be buried, but to be lived; to bear fruit that will endure (John 15:16).

## *Gift Of Fear Of The Lord*

A strange gift, it would seem. Yet the psalmist speaks, "Holy is His name, commanding our awe. The fear of the Lord is the beginning of wisdom. They have sound sense who practise it" (Psalm 111:10). In early scriptures fear implied holy terror, taking off the shoes, prostration and the adoration of fear. It was the recognition of a presence superior to himself before which man was reduced to insignificance. The later Hebrew Scriptures no longer imply physical fear in the presence of God's power, but rather a reverence and wonder, a humble heart and the adoration of love. This fear is beautifully expressed in *Sirach* 1:

> "The fear of the Lord is glory and pride
> and happiness and a crown of joyfulness . . .
> The fear of the Lord is the perfection of
> wisdom
> she intoxicates them with her fruits . . .
> The fear of the Lord is the crown of wisdom
> it makes peace and health to flourish . . . .

Jeremiah foretold the new covenant which was to restore the "fear of God" in a new heart. "I will make them a different heart and different behavior so that they will always fear me, for the good of themselves and their children after them" (Jeremiah 32:39).

There are two aspects of Biblical fear, one referring to the holiness and goodness of God, the other to man's sinfulness and ingratitude. Through His love unto death, Christ has overcome the fear that comes because we have sinned. "Love will come to perfection in us when we can face the day of Judgment without fear, because even in this world we have become as He is. In love there can be no fear, for perfect love casts out fear. To fear is to expect punishment, and anyone who is still afraid is still imperfect in love" (1 John 4:17).

There will be, nonetheless, always an appropriate fear of God which is a gift of the Spirit – the awe and reverence and wonder before the gift of His love. Mary in the *Magnificat* speaks of this fear: "Holy is his name, and his mercy reaches from age to age for those *who fear him*" (Luke 1:50). It echoes the psalm, "Yet Yahweh's love for those *who fear him* lasts from all eternity and forever" (Psalm 103:17).

In the first petition of the Our Father, "Hallowed be thy name," is implicit the demand of fear and reverence before the incredible love of the Father who so loved the world that He sent his Son to us. Hallowed by thy love; cherished, recalled, never to be forgotten. Paradoxically, what we most fear is love. Our enemies can neither ask nor get anything from us – we are comfortable because we can maintain our autonomy. If, however, someone loves us completely, abandons oneself totally to us, then we are no longer our own. Love evokes love. "Where there is no love, put love, and you will find it." Often we try to insulate ourselves against such love because it asks the same in return. Partial love we can handle, but total love begets a running fear in us; instinctively, we hide.

"Who is that
Figure
walking
by the waters,
along the shore
white, shining,
and terrible?
He
looks
at me with
Knowing eyes
that hurt.
I
think
He sees
my every fiber
with those
Eyes . . .
glowing
blazing
probing
loving
Eyes,
dreadful
asking Eyes.
They say
straightforward
nothing less
than all
of you
is what
I want."

Fear of the Lord is fear of His love, fear of his generosity, of His asking. God's weakness is man. Man's weakness is God. He makes such a gift of himself to us that we become His gift to others. We discover that we are most ourselves when we are His and therefore belong to others.

## *Gift of Piety* — **of filial fidelity.**

"Piety" is a word which has become emasculated and disemboweled. It has been reversed in meaning, now often suggesting "marked by sham or hypocrisy" or "marked by self-conscious virtue." To refer to someone as pious is not to be complimentary. Originally, piety was a strong good word, signifying fidelity, loyalty, responsibility, integrity. In its natural sense it expressed a sense of duty and indebtedness to parents and family, indicating what parents should be able to expect from their children, and how children wished to respond to parents. It carried the spirit of "noblesse oblige."

As a gift of the Spirit, it calls upon us to know who we are, whose we are, and what we are called upon to be — "not servants but sons." It enjoins upon us a filial duty, fidelity, integrity. "The Spirit you received is not the spirit of slaves, bringing fear into your lives again; it is the spirit of sons, making us cry out, "Abba, Father" (Romans 8:15). The psalmist asks our question, "What return can I make to Yahweh for all his goodness to me?" and answers it, "I will walk in Yahweh's presence" (Psalm 116:12). The answer is an echo of words in Leviticus, "Be consecrated to me because I, Yahweh, am holy" (Leviticus 20:26). And this is validated for all time in the Sermon on the Mount, "You must therefore be perfect just as your heavenly Father is perfect" (Matthew 5:48).

This deep sense of the gift of piety is expressed throughout the Scriptures, by the prophets and the apostles:

> Be holy in all you do, since it is the Holy One who has called you, and Scripture says: Be holy for I am holy (I Peter 1:15). You are a chosen race, a royal priesthood, a consecrated nation, a holy people set apart to sing the praise of God who called you out of darkness into His wonderful light (I Peter 2:9).

> No one who has been begotten by God sins because God's spirit remains within him (I John 3:9).

Piety, the gift of the Holy Spirit, leads us from the Father to a sense of fraternity with all men. Jesus prayed, "for their sake I consecrate myself that they, too, may be consecrated in truth" (John 17:17).

In Paul's letters, we have the strong sense of parenthood, of responsibility which he feels for those whom he has taught:

> You are yourselves our letter, written in our heart, that anyone can see and read, and it is plain that you are a letter from Christ; drawn up by us, and written not with ink but with the Spirit of the living God, not on

stone tablets but on the tablets of your living hearts (II Co. 3:2,3).

You might have thousands of guardians in Christ, but not more than one father; and it was I who begot you in Christ Jesus by preaching the Good News. That is why I beg you to copy me. (I Co. 4:15).

We have spoken to you very frankly; our mind has been opened in front of you. I speak as if to children of mine: as a fair exchange, open your mind in the same way. . . .

Like a mother feeding and looking after her own children, we felt so devoted and pro-tective toward you, and had come to love you so much that we were eager to hand over to you not only the Good News but our whole lives as well (I Th. 2:8).

The Gift of Piety is lifted from the natural duty and fidelity in the human realm to the spiritual dimension of our call to faithful-ness and responsibility as the children of God; of those who have heard the Word, been called to be sons and daughters of the Most High.

### *Gift Of Courage*

Courage is the gift of the Spirit which is immediately identified with the sacrament of Confirmation. "You will receive *power* when the Holy Spirit comes on you and then you will be *my witnesses*" (Acts 1:8). To be witnesses was to speak the Word, and that speaking carried with it the need of courage. The ultimate witness might mean martyrdom, and for that they were to hold themselves in readiness, to be fearless as Jesus was fearless. In our own century, Charles de Foucauld clearly manifested the gift of courage when, in the early days of his ministry, he wrote, and constantly carried with him, the words, "Remember that you will die by violence and in pain . . . and hope it will be today."

Courage is the gift of perseverance, of life-long commitment, of total discipleship. Carefully Our Lord instructed his disciples concerning the cost of this discipleship, their weakness and their need of the Spirit. "Without me, you are nothing" (John 15:5) He told them. Yet they, like Paul, would grow in strength and courage, be able to say with him, "I can do all things through Christ who strengthens me" (Ph. 4:14).

It is when we become conscious of our weakness that we are able to receive the power of the Holy Spirit. "He chose what is weak by human reckoning to shame what is strong" (I Co 4:7). Repeatedly, Paul realized that the power of the Spirit in him revealed itself most strongly in his weakness. "I am happy," he said, "to make my weakness my special boast so that the power of Christ may stay over me. That is

why I am quite content with my weak-
nesses, and with insults, hardships, persecu-
tions, and the agonies I go through for
Christ's sake. For it is when I am weak that
I am strong" (2 Co 12:9).

The gift of courage is not bestowed by
the Spirit merely for the ordinary human
struggle. *"For it is not against human
enemies alone that we have to struggle,* but
against the Sovereignties and the Power
who originate the darkness in this world,
the spiritual army of evil in the heavens.
This is why you must rely on God's armor,
or you will not be able to put up any
resistance when the worst happens, or have
enough resources to stand your ground"
(Ephesians 5:10).

The letter to the Hebrews is a ringing call
to remember the faith and courage of those
who handed the faith to us. "With so many
witnesses in a great cloud on every side of
us, we too, then, should throw off everything that hinders us, especially the sin that
clings so easily, and keep running steadily
in the race we have started. Let us not lose
sight of Jesus, who leads us in our faith and
brings it to perfection: for the sake of the
joy which was still in the future, he
endured the cross, disregarding the shame-
fulness of it, and *from now on has taken
his place at the right* of God's throne.
Think of the way he stood such opposition
from sinners and then you will not give up
for want of courage. In the fight against
sin, you have not yet had to keep fighting

to the point of death" (Hebrews 12:1-4).
"For our God is a consuming fire"
(Hebrews 12:29).

Peter, too, breathes courage and hope in
his letter. "Bow down, then, before the
power of God now, and he will raise you
up on the appointed day; *unload all your
worries on to him,* since he is looking after
you. *Be calm but vigilant,* because your
enemy the devil is prowling round like a
roaring lion, looking for someone to eat.
Stand up to him, strong in faith and in the
knowledge that your brothers all over the
world are suffering the same things. You
will have to suffer only for a little while:
the God of all grace who called you to
eternal glory in Christ will see that all is
well again: he will confirm, strengthen and
support you. His power lasts for ever and
ever. Amen" (I Peter 5:6-11).

The gift of courage enables one to live
out the truth of the beatitude, "Blessed are
those who are persecuted in the cause of
right" (Matthew 5:10).

One can avoid the kind of persecution
of which Christ spoke by simply walking
away from Him. "What about you," He
asked his disciples as the crowds were
dispersing, leaving Him, "do you want to
go away too?" (John 6:67). He knew of
His own coming Passion. He knew, too,
that to be His disciple was to take up His
cross every day, to renounce oneself, and
to follow Him; even to death.

"If anyone wants to be a follower of

mine, let him renounce himself and take up his cross every day and follow me. For anyone who wants to save his life will lose it; but anyone who loses his life for my sake, that man will save it" (Luke 9:23-24). The phrase "take up his cross" does not mean our generalized notion of mortification and self-denial. It means, literally, prepare yourself for criminal execution, be ready to die today. The gift of courage to enable one to live out this beatitude is, it should again and again be emphasized, the capacity to identify with Christ, to suffer ultimate suffering in the cause of His righteousness. It is not the imaginary nor the neurotic suffering we bring upon ourselves because we are a cross to other people.

The Book of Wisdom underlines the deep need we have to receive the gift of courage from the Holy Spirit:

> Let us lie in wait for the virtuous man,
> since he annoys
> us and opposes our way of life,
> reproaches us for our breaches of the law
> and accuses us of playing false to our
> upbringing . . .
> the very sight of him weighs our spirits
> down;
> his way of life is not like other men's,
> the paths he treads are unfamiliar.
> In his opinion we are counterfeit;
> he holds aloof from our doings as though
> from filth; . . .
> Let us test with cruelty and with torture,

and thus explore this gentleness of his
and put his endurance to the proof.
Let us condemn him to a shameful death
since he will be looked after — we have his
    word for it (Wisdom 2:12).

## *Gift Of Counsel*

When we speak of the seven gifts of the
Holy Spirit, this is not a numerical term.
The gifts of the Holy Spirit are not
numberable. Even in the scriptural passage
from Isaiah about the seven gifts, the fear
of God and piety probably form one word.
Literally, then, there are not seven gifts.
There are as many gifts of the Holy Spirit
as there are people. One way of looking at
the multiple graces of the Holy Spirit is
that they have different specifications.
Counsel is probably one of the more elusive
of the gifts of the Holy Spirit. I think of
counsel in terms of discernment. While it
cannot be separated from wisdom or understanding or knowledge or holiness, it has its
own particular focus. The more human way
of looking at it is in terms of prudence, of
common sense, which is really uncommon.

    I hope there will be an increasing focus
on discernment because this seems to be
one of the great needs of our day, a day
when there is less and less structure, less
and less outside direction. As we grow into
a greater and greater personal freedom, we
need all the more the discernment of

spirits. It is of the utmost importance. We pray for it so often in the Our Father, "Thy will be done," but the question we must ask is, "What is His will this particular day for me in this particular situation?"

John, in both his gospel and in his epistle, writes, "If you want to know, you will know." Although that is a real promise, yet we feel a certain elusiveness in it. One of our problems is that each of us lives more or less encased in the cell of our own existence. In any particular day we can cover only so much ground. We are immediately aware of our limitations. How far can we see? Relatively not far; nor can we hear at great distances. What a small pocket of experience is ours from day to day, our immediate tangible experience. When you think of it, we are a very small limited cell of consciousness, and one of our particular problems is how we relate, how we hold together the flow of our life from yesterday to today and from today until tomorrow. How do we keep track of the movement and direction of our life. If we cannot do it for our own life, how do we dare hope we can help those who constantly turn to us for discernment, for direction, for guidance. There is a need, as the sailors used to say, to "shoot the sun," to learn how to take one's bearings.

In the old days we used to insist upon the examen of conscience which often was a negative way of looking at how one had sinned. More and more the direction has become an examen of *consciousness.* How conscious are we of ourselves, of others, of what is happening to us? It is much more positive thinking, of consciousness or sensitivity, of awareness, or of simply being present. We must learn how to be present to ourselves, present to others, present to what is.

Discernment is not something which is achieved once and for all. Perhaps it is somewhat inaccurate to use the term *"discernment* of spirits" as if we can do it once and be finished with it. It is rather the ongoing *discerning* heart, the Spirit-guided insight into life. How has the Lord been working in us? What has he been asking — not necessarily what have we been doing. There is a gap between what we have been doing and what He has been saying, what He has been asking and how we have discerned it, been aware of it. This is why in meditation we should try to remember, to call to mind what the Spirit has been doing. What are the *actions* of our lives, not just the thoughts and ideas because many times our eyes are far ahead of our feet. We have to look at what we have done, not only at what we have thought or of what we have hoped. Sometimes we do not recognize the facts of our life. It is difficult to make a review of life, to look at the facts of one's life distinct from ideas and thoughts.

The gift of discernment is to "let happen that beautiful spontaneity in our hearts which is the touch of our Father, the urging of the Spirit." There is a very delicate nuance here. The touch of the Father, the urging of the Spirit. There is only one way God can approach us and that is freely — never in a way that compels, never in a way in which we cannot be free because if there is anything that is not free, then it cannot be for Him. Only in love is the touch of the Father, the urging of the Spirit and a delicate discerning responsiveness. What we need is a "passionate receptivity," a passionate receptivity to the gentle breeze, the gentle wind, the gentle touch, the gentle urging. There is always some "area of our heart which is especially calling for conversion, where there is the beginning of the new life."

Ignatius was more reluctant to omit his examen of consciousness than his formal contemplative prayer each day. He would forego his contemplative prayer, if necessary, in order to have that examen of consciousness; to put himself in the presence of the Father, a Father who looked at him on this particular day. There is in the Old Testament the beautiful call to be in the presence of God, to walk before Him, to see how He looks upon us this particular day and to see all things in the sight of God.

This act of consciousness, this act of discernment is intimately connected with our growing identity. The discerning is the discerning of our own self, what is happening in our life, how our identity is unfolding and, of course, finding God in all things, at all times. Prayer always leads us to a deeper discerning of how we are before God and how He is leading us. The hope of any prayerful life is at every moment the loving discovery of God in the existential situation of our life. Our prayer never ends in itself but is to enable us to be in joy and peace and in deep quiet wherever we find ourselves. It is because He is always with us and we have always a sense of His presence to us.

### Gift Of Knowledge

Scripture has much to say to us of knowledge. In Psalm 139 the omnipresence of God is made clear, His omniscience, His knowledge of the individual. "You know if I am standing or sitting," says the Psalmist, "You read my thoughts from far away. Whether I walk or lie down, You are watching. You know every detail of my conduct. Where could I go to escape Your Spirit? Where could I flee from Your presence? If I climb the heavens, You are there. There too, if I lie in sheol."

And in Paul's letter to the Romans, he speaks of the riches and the depths of God: "How deep His wisdom and knowledge, how impossible to penetrate or understand Him." " 'Who could ever know the mind of

the Lord or who could ever be His counsel-
or"?" he quotes.

In Psalm 119, the great psalm of the
covenant, we find the statement of the law,
the knowledge of the law, its effect upon
life if one observes it. A magnificent psalm,
meriting prayerful and repeated study.

There are different kinds of knowledge,
of course, even as there are differing gifts
of the Spirit. There is the knowledge we
gain from books. In a far different sense,
there is the Old Testament knowledge
which one possesses when he has a union
with it. The Hebrew notion of truth was
not conceptual; it did not consider that
anything was known unless it was directly
and immediately experienced. Truth for
the Hebrew was as objective as a rock and
it was of that kind of experience they
spoke when they talked of knowledge.
There is a difference to them between a
notion and real assent. One really does not
possess knowledge without some kind of
experience. Conceptual knowledge alone is
not considered full knowledge. And in our
reading of the Scriptures, particularly of
the Old Testament, we should keep this in
mind.

Apart from these rather expository no-
tions of knowledge, there is communicable
knowledge and that which is incommuni-
cable. There is knowledge one can pass on
to someone else and that which can remain
only within oneself. There is knowledge in
the midst of progress and growth, the idea

of growing on from grace to grace, involving knowledge, from truth to truth through knowledge. In the New Testament, Paul brings together the three gifts of the Holy Spirit, perfect wisdom, spiritual understanding and fullness of knowledge. The Letter to the Ephesians, especially, is centered upon wisdom and understanding and knowledge. Paul's conviction is that we have a hidden self, hidden even from ourselves which becomes alive and is born only through our contact with Christ. "Try to discover," Paul urges his hearers, "what the Lord wants of you." This, of course, is related to discernment. Again Paul says that one does not really *know* until he knows God's secret. This knowledge, which is through meditation, contemplation and affective prayer, indicates that he believes it is one thing to read scripture, but it is far different to know it.

Man has been described as a rational, knowing animal but I think perhaps a better way of expressing it is that man is a learner who has an infinite capacity for knowledge, curiosity, wonder and praise. From the time we are infants we are led to fuller knowledge simply out of curiosity, out of wonder. This is true not only on the human material level but also on the spiritual one. How little we know even of the world around us. And, yet knowing as little as we do even of our physical environment, we are called to this still deeper knowledge, this mysterious knowledge of

God on a spiritual level. The Book of Wisdom speaks about the mystery of our understanding so little of what is around us, yet our feeling the constant call to know God.

We know, too, how we try to avoid acquiring this knowledge. We do not want to know too much of Him. All of us find in ourselves the Hound of Heaven syndrome. "Where ignorance is bliss, 'tis folly to be wise," suggests that we know that the more we know, the more we are responsible for. We do not handle the knowledge we have now, we sometimes think, so why go on? Yet there is always the temptation of knowledge. We do tend to believe that wisdom will come with the next book we read or the next retreat we make. It is "tomorrow," "tomorrow." Our conviction that there is salvation through knowledge, or in the gnosticism of today that there is salvation through theology or through scripture or even through asceticism. On the contrary St. Paul, I think, says it most deeply when he says, "I know Him in whom I believe." This is the kind of knowledge which is the gift of the Spirit. The gifts of the Spirit are activations of the theological gifts of faith, hope and charity, the activation which keeps them alive, keeps them growing. It might be well to note what gifts of knowledge we have already received; curiosity; the people who have spurred us on; teachers we have had; the sacrament of the Word. Above all is the call of the Spirit to enter more deeply, even through suffering, into the knowledge of the love of God which is in Christ Jesus our Lord.

## *Gift Of Understanding*

In His last days with His disciples Jesus spoke to them about the Holy Spirit. "I will give you another Counselor to be with you forever," He told them, "the Spirit of truth. You know because He is with you, He is in you." "I still have many things to say to you but that would be too much for you now. But when the Spirit of truth comes he will lead you to the complete truth." This is the ongoing action of Christ through the Holy Spirit to make the Father known to us. The work of the Spirit is to teach us one word, "Abba," and the whole work of Jesus is to teach us who His Father is.

Sometimes we tend to think that all the work of learning, of knowing, of under standing depends upon ourselves, that our whole spiritual life is something we our- selves can achieve. In one sense this may be true but the real accomplishment, the real achievement is the gift of Christ. "I have given them the teaching You gave to me." We are responsible then for handing Christ on. If we do not allow ourselves to be open to the Spirit then we give to others an incomplete Christ, a partial Christ. Our need is to be very much in tune with the Spirit so that we give the full measure, all we are capable of giving, the full measure of our own understanding of Christ which we have achieved through our listening and through our prayer.

The question Our Lord repeated many times throughout the Gospels is, "Do you understand what I have done to you?" "Do you understand what I am doing to you?" When He speaks about being the Way, the Truth and the Life, He is speaking of Himself as a teacher and the work of a teacher is to have those whom he teaches understand. "At this moment," He said, "you do not know what I am doing, but later you will understand." "I, the Light, have come into the world so that whoever believes in Me need not stay in the dark any more." "You have been anointed by the Holy One and have received the knowledge." These are words of great depth over which we tend not to pause long enough really to capture the depth of their meaning.

There is a total reality of faith as understanding, of power. Understanding does indeed mean power and this is Paul's basic theme, the Word of God as power, as creative, as rendering Christ present. It might be good for us to try to write down our own gifts of understanding, what the faith insights are which are uniquely our own. We may be able to feel awed by the presence shining through the presence of others. An expanding personal universe of faith may come upon us with an awareness of revelation, or we may understand in a new way the progression of our faith. If our faith is static then it is atrophied, no longer alive.

We do have to learn to accept the limitations of our own understanding. Even as the disciples were not able to understand, we cannot understand what the future holds. Sometimes it seems to us we understand nothing. Why does this particular event occur? Why has this happened to us? What is this mystery of the time which we spend with God? Let us remember that when something new comes into our lives it could not have happened at any other time or in any other place. Let us be open and small and waiting for the gift of understanding.

There are those who draw the grace of understanding from us if we are open. At times people ask questions which we cannot answer until the moment they ask us. And when we answer we discover in the very process of answering what we never knew ourselves, or at least what we had never reflectively understood. Someone has asked me a question which I have never heard in my life before, and in the very asking of the question I come, out of necessity, to an insight. It is given to me at that moment and I have an understanding that was not there. There are times when some counsel which you have given to another is returned to you a year or so later with a far richer understanding than you had when you gave it to them. It is a beautiful grace that sometimes people understand you far better than you understand yourself. One of the words in the English language to be cherished is, "I understand," the understanding which comes from joy, from love. There is a vast difference between acquired understanding and the gift of God, of the Holy Spirit, which does not come from study. It comes from an intuition which is not of ourselves.

All of this understanding is related to the mysterious action of the Spirit in us far beyond anything which we can do or acquire or anything which we may achieve by our own effort. We must remember always, however, that it is not given to us without our openness, our receptivity and our will to understand, to pray, to live with God, to move toward Him, to move inward with Him to a deep and full understanding, to achieve through His grace all the understanding of which we are capable.

### Gift of Wisdom

Paul in his letter to the Corinthians says of Christ, "He is our wisdom, our power, our courage and our holiness." The wisdom of the Holy Spirit is to bring us to the full measure of Christ. To acquire wisdom is a life-long process, a truth reflected in many passages of scripture. In the Book of Wisdom we find it in Solomon's anticipation of Christ and the outpouring of the Spirit. "It is hard enough for us to work out what is on earth, laborious to know what lies within our reach; who, then, can discover what is in the heavens? As for your intention, who could have learnt it, had you not granted wisdom and sent your holy spirit from above?" Luke speaks of Christ's own growth in wisdom, "And Jesus increased in wisdom, in stature, and in favor with God and men." One of the questions of speculative theology in terms of Christ's human understanding is, "At what moment did Jesus know in his human personality that he was Christ?" And we might ask ourselves at what moment have we realized that we could be Christ — that in a very real sense, we are Christ. When have we been aware of the mystery of identity between Christ and ourselves, of our growing into this wisdom, our growing into this reality. It is not something of the mind; there is the actuality of His grace, of His Spirit growing in us. Paul contrasts the foolishness of human wisdom with the foolishness of the cross.

What is true of the gift of understanding is true also of wisdom; it is the hidden wisdom of God, the hidden mystery, "The revelation of the mystery kept secret for endless ages." Paul returns constantly to the theme, "He alone is our wisdom." How deep is Christ's wisdom, His wisdom and knowledge. His wisdom is a grand canyon which we shall never wholly explore. He is the ocean which we see in so limited a way, the heavens which fill us with awe and praise.

Job asks, "Can you grasp the mystery of God?" Paul says wisdom is the "power through the Spirit for the hidden self to grow strong." I think it is good to reflect upon what has happened in us to see if we can discern how the Spirit of Wisdom has worked in us and what the particular gift of the Spirit is which has been actualized in us from our life circumstances, from the people with whom we are in contact, and what remains to be activated more fully. The Holy Spirit is not given to us in terms merely of ourselves but He is always given in order to effect community. The Acts of the Apostles mentions the mystery of the Christian community, how they shared everything they had — they sold all they had and shared it together — not only materially but also spiritually. All that is given us is for us to use to enrich one another, to give to one another the gift of wisdom. The mystery of the gift of wisdom is much in demand in the church today, the mystery of community. We are only now coming of age. Can the church make it? A community becomes a parable; it becomes an image of the totality of the church.

What death must yet be undergone by each one in order that the whole Chirst may be formed?

So I think there is a need to pray for forgiveness for the sins against the Holy Spirit in each person because there is much in each one of us that has not yet died; there is much in us that has not yet risen. There is much that the Spirit must do in us to give us spiritual wisdom. It must be done by the whole church, by everyone calling down, almost imposing hands on one another so that the work of the Spirit may be done and continue to be done in ourselves so that it can be done in the church and in the world. We are individually and collectively the church. If we do not pray for the gift of wisdom, if we do not truly and deeply understand "the foolishness of the cross," which is God's wisdom, then we shall not grow as we are called to do.

The gift of wisdom, a gift of the Holy Spirit, requires of us deep reflection on the meaning of our life experiences, a commitment to listen with humility, to learn, to give to others of the wisdom entrusted to us through the love of Christ in the Holy Spirit.

## IV DISCIPLESHIP

To read carefully the gospel account of Jesus' ministry is to become aware of His continuous association with His small group of disciples. He chose them. "Having spent the night in prayer," He called them; and from that time forth was engaged in their formation and training. Far too limited a consideration has been given to what we can learn of the meaning of discipleship from Jesus' disciples. They were, viewed objectively, a somewhat unlikely lot. They remained relatively obtuse, narrow in vision and understanding, dominated by dreams of earthly glory. And, in the end, they left Jesus to His lonely suffering.

Yet we think of these disciples as forming in a real sense a model for us. This fact leads us to consider our own understanding of what it means to be disciples of Jesus, what is implied in discipleship.

Disciple and discipline are from the same root. In order to be a disciple one accepts a certain discipline, enters into a particular style of life. If one accepts the call of Christ, he learns how difficult it is to be His follower. How easily, consciously and unconsciously, we are instead our own good servants; how easily we confuse self-service and self-ministry with service and ministry to Him. Many times we set out to do good and end "doing well." In the midst of our activity we tend to lose sight of what we committed ourselves to do. Disillusionment follows our failure, and the result is both confusion and loss of direction.

It is good to be amazed at both the arrogance and the naiveté that we experience in ourselves in our effort to follow Jesus, to commit our will to God. How easy it is to use God, to reduce Him to being our servant, our disciple, our witness. I think we all find ourselves sometimes saying in our prayer, "My will be done, my kingdom come." This is part of our human limitation. There is, however, no limit which can be set to our discipleship of Jesus — no one can prevent us from being holy, from being in interior union with Him. This is something we alone condition. While this is true, there are limits to our exterior servanthood and apostolate. Many circumstances, and many people can interfere with this apostolate, for in it our freedom is limited by every other person, even as our freedom in our horizontal relationships is limited by every other person. We have no more authority than they choose to give us.

Discipleship costs. In the command Jesus gave to his disciples to feed the multitude, to "Give them something to eat yourselves," is shown symbolically that they were to be broken, to be distributed, to be eaten. This is the centrality of the Eucharist in our ministry — the giving of ourselves. We must be broken. We must give ourselves to him. Only He can break us and distribute us and make us His bread. In the end, it is only the Lord Himself who can teach us to be disciples. Jesus commands, not with mere words but by His life. The only authority He has, that He has exercised in each of our lives is to create in us the desire to be what He is and to use our life as He used His life. Eventually His first disciples learned what He had taught them when He was with them.

He commanded, "Go and teach all men. Make disciples of all men." What a tremendous responsibility that is. Be very careful what you teach them; they may learn it. Rahner makes a rather frightening statement in one of the dictionaries of dogmatic theology. He writes that atheism can be created by someone preaching the gospel who does not believe in it. He said in addition that this is not uncommon; a truth which was reflected in the Vatican II Document on the Church in the Modern World. The Christian bears responsibility or culpability in creating atheism — by mouthing that which he does not live. "Love as I have loved you." The youth culture confronts verbal love with some cynicism. When you say "I love you," they fire back, "I feel no difference in me because of your love; I see no difference in you because you love me." Often, they speak truly.

Jesus said to Peter, "I will make you a fisher of men." Only Jesus can make us fishers of men; we cannot make ourselves powerful. We must learn to be disciples of one another, to learn, to admire, and to grow. How we become disciples to one another is an important question. What have we learned from another? What have we received? How do we give grace to another? And in our relationshp to Jesus what does it mean that he is the Lord, that he is Master? To what extent do we call him Lord and how much power do we let him have over us? When it comes down to it, the significant question for us all is, "How do we make our decisions?" These are difficult questions to answer, yet they are valid questions demanding honest response. How do we listen to Jesus? How do we obey him? Christ spoke often of obedience, and the basic principle of His own decisions was obedience to the Father. Obedience is difficult for us; etymologically it means listening. Do we really listen, really seek his presence, acknowledge Him as the Teacher, the Master of our whole life?

The discipline involved in discipleship makes the difference between the child and the man, the girl and the woman, the receiver and the giver, the dying and rising, the "no" of sacrifice and the "yes" of oblation. Decision is also an exclusion; it means that options are closed, alternatives are no longer available – the middle ground is excluded. In other words, those who try to attain the best of both worlds usually end up with the worst of both. Unless a man dies, then, there is no birth, no maturity – no ability to work, to suffer, to labor, to bear in the body his wounds. We cannot be his disciples if our lives contradict His life.

## V SURPRISED BY THE SPIRIT

*"The depths of a man can only be known by his own spirit, not by any other man, and in the same way the depths of God can only be known by the Spirit of God" (1 Co. 2, 11).*

*"Now instead of the spirit of the world, we have received the Spirit that comes from God, to teach us to understand the gifts that He has given us" (1 Co. 2, 12).*

Constantly in the Eucharistic prayers there is brought before our minds and hearts the presence and power of the Holy Spirit:

and that we might live no longer for
ourselves but for him
he sent the Holy Spirit from you, Father,
as his first gift to those who believe,
to complete his work on earth
and bring us the fulness of grace.

Each of the Eucharistic Prayers calls down the presence and power of the Spirit, prays for the power of the Holy Spirit:

II Let your Spirit come upon these gifts
to make them holy.
III We ask you to make them holy by the
power of your spirit.
IV May this Holy Spirit sanctify these offer-
ings.

These prayers create a fresh consciousness of the Holy Spirit. Yet it is difficult to write or speak of the Holy Spirit. We are rather hesitant to claim the Spirit as "ours" in spite of our ease in praying "our" Father, "our" Lord, "my" Jesus. There is a reserve, a humbleness, a muteness before the Spirit. Perhaps it is the adjective "Holy" prefixed to the Spirit that makes us reluctant to say "our" Holy Spirit, "my" Holy Spirit. To say "Father" or "Son" is to speak in terms of definite, clear, human images and correlatives having some tangible reference. The Spirit does not lend Himself to such tangible human categories, descriptions or definitions. Our vocabulary, our language, even our theology clouds the Spirit and conceals more than reveals. Light cannot be put into a bushel or the ocean into a bucket. It is the Spirit which gives life to the word; the word itself is often deadly.

The Spirit is elusive, unobtrusive, as imperceptible as time and season, growth and age. Yet man has a deep sense of Spirit from the breath of his life, the pulse of his heart, the stirring of his conscience, the restlessness of his soul. In this, modern man is not far removed from primitive man. Aloneness, silence, darkness, sleep, and death touch us too deeply to allow us to forget the mystery of the absolute. How intuitive ancient man was in sensing that the Spirit was in all things.

The Spirit draws no attention to himself. "He will not be speaking as from Himself" (John 16, 13). The Spirit has no personal name, no new message, no Gospel. In fact, the Spirit has only one word to say to us and that is the *seed* word of Jesus' whole gospel, the deepest word He taught us: Abba, my dearly beloved Father. The Spirit belongs to the Father and the Son; He exists as the totality of their love for each other. He is "ours" only in relation to them as their gift to us drawing us into the eternal interflow of their mutual love and life. In all the universe only man can be tempted not to love, to exist for himself. The Spirit brought to understanding what Jesus said, that God is love and does not exist for himself but for the Son and the Son for the Father, and this love is the person of the Spirit who is now poured into our hearts by the Father and Son. The Incarnation has saturated and *densified* the whole cosmos with the Spirit, who is far more real and actual than anything physical or sensate. He is immanent because transcendent.

The paradox of the Spirit is that we do not possess Him, rather that He possesses us, occupies us. We become "His," not He "ours." We are a grain of sand wanting to possess the ocean. He is the ocean that encompasses us. Yet for that incredible lifetime of Jesus, the ocean was contained in a human grain of sand. "For there was no Spirit as yet because Jesus had not yet been glorified" (John 7, 39). The spirit was only in Jesus and was released only through his suffering, dying and being consumed.

As Christ was lifted up in death and glory, the Spirit poured from His open side in water and blood to baptize and recreate the face of the earth. The Holy Spirit is the Spirit of Jesus now given to us to enable us to love with His love, to die in His death, to give our body and blood for others, to consecrate as He commanded which is to love one another as He loved us. The great manifestation of the Spirit each day is the power and presence to say in liturgy and in life, "This is *my* body, this is *my* blood."

The Holy Spirit must be, then, more than the once-in-a-life-time experience of the Sacrament of Confirmation or the once-a-year commemoration of Pentecost. In Jesus' farewell discourse He said that He would ask the Father to give us another helper to be with us forever. "The Advocate, the Holy Spirit, whom the Father will send in my name, will *teach* you everything and remind you of all I have said to you" (John 14, 26). "When the Spirit of truth comes He will *lead* you to the complete truth" (John 16, 11).

The more one tries to study and understand the Spirit, the more difficulties one encounters. The Spirit seems to defy definition and even description. No categories can contain Him. His manifestations are beyond computing. Many are His forms, His faces, His guises – breath, dove, wind, fire, water, power, unity, witness, discernment, are words used in the effort to capture His essence. The activity of the Spirit ranges from creation and wisdom in the Old Testament to Incarnation and Resurrection in the New. The Gifts, Fruits, Beatitudes are His. The whole of creation is charged with His presence, unobtrusive yet irresistibly penetrating and expanding. The Spirit is a holy seducer and a divine tempter. It is evident beyond any doubt that he is plotting to make us holy and happy. This "finger of God," "Hound of heaven" uses every opening, excuse, subterfuge, even our sin, to complete the work begun in us by Jesus.

The Spirit is inner transformation, being born again. The Spirit stirs up, prods, lifts up; never sleeps, is persistent, wears us down, ever returns. "You hear its sound, but cannot tell where it comes from or where it is going." He has His own way of revealing Himself. He is always *surprise.* When we least suspect it, He is breathing in us. He awakens us, recreates a forgotten appetite, stirs up a lost hunger and thirst, gifts us with an energy, a facility, a freedom and "unites us to the Lord to make with Him one Spirit" (1 Co. 6:17).

The Holy Spirit is inclusive, all embracing, community-creating. He comes upon us not for ourselves privately but to enable us to *be* for others, to build up the Body. He builds the kingdom between us. He breaks down the strangeness, removes the barriers, and bridges the estrangement created by the cumulative sin of man. He enables us to perceive and discern the truth and light in each person. Our immediate rash judgments of others are countered by his unconditioned love and reverence for each person. We become open to the gift of the Spirit in the stranger, to what may be lacking on one level being present on another. We begin to know what we see, in place of seeing only what we know. Instead of seeing only the outside, we develop *insight* and see from within.

We must be constantly aware, however, that life in the Spirit depends upon our faith exercised in the Spirit and our response acted out in charity. The harvest of the Spirit comes from using His gifts and from living the beatitudes. How much we have yet to learn from Mary's great hymn to the Spirit, the *Magnificat.* Our emptiness is filled with the Spirit. Only the Spirit can lead us into the charity Paul describes in his letter to the Corinthians and the Christian style of life he describes in his letter to the Romans:

> "Bless those who persecute you: never curse them, bless them. Rejoice with those who rejoice and be sad with those in sorrow. Treat everyone with equal kindness; never be condescending but make real friends with the poor. Do not allow yourself to become self-satisfied. Never repay evil with evil but let everyone see that you are interested only in the highest ideals. Do all you can to live at

peace with everyone. Never try to get revenge; leave that, my friends, to God's anger. As scripture says: 'Vengeance is mine — I will pay them back,' the Lord promises. But there is more: 'If your enemy is hungry, you should give him food, and if he is thirsty, let him drink. Thus you heap red-hot coals on his head.' Resist evil and conquer it with good" (Romans 12:14-21).

The Beatitudes and the works of mercy in Matthew 25 enter our lives only by the power and gentleness of the Spirit. The Spirit has to be poured into our hearts if we are to make Paul's hymn to the Spirit a description of our own love, "Always patient and kind/never jealous/never boastful or conceited/never rude or selfish/not taking offense/not resentful/no pleasure in others' sin/delights in the truth/always ready to excuse/to trust, to hope/to endure whatever comes."

"The Spirit comes to help us in our weakness. For when we cannot choose words in order to pray properly, the Spirit himself expresses our plea in a way that could never be put into words, and God who knows everything in our hearts knows perfectly well what he means." So must we pray that our hidden selves may grow strong until knowing "the love of Christ which is beyond all knowledge you are filled with the utter fulness (pleroma) of God" (Ephesians 3:16).

# VI CELTIC MEDITATION EXERCISES

"I AM                          *Exercise in Adoration.*
with you."

Prayer essentially is to become present to oneself, to God, to all of reality. It is not easy to become present to oneself, to be fully conscious, to be totally awake. Practice, training, exercise are necessary to discover oneself, to receive the gift of oneself. We are so caught up in events and with the people in our lives that we rarely take time to consider our own selves to be worth any time at all. To take time for ourselves also triggers some guilt in us. Yet only if we are free to "waste" time on ourselves are we truly free. The closest reality to God that one will ever experience is oneself. Each of us is an existence of God, a presence of Christ, a sacrament of the church, a gift to the world. Bonhoeffer expresses it: "if you refuse to be with yourself alone you are rejecting Christ's call to you."

Each of us needs a "peace center," a place where we can be most ourselves, a home that welcomes us no matter how we are or what we have done. It can be a cottage, a park, a mountain, woods, a chapel. As life goes on we find different peace centers. When we most need our geographical peace center, however, time and the situation sometimes render it impossible. We are compelled to create our peace center within ourselves. Jesus had to leave Nazareth, yet He always carried it within Himself. Each of us has to create our hermitage and oasis within, our Nazareth, our Bethany.

*Let us begin!*

Close your eyes and sit as erect as possible, your feet flat on the ground and your hands on your lap, palms up, without touching each other. A straight-backed chair is best; lounge chairs actually make the body restless.

Begin to be aware of your breathing. Tune into the sensation of your whole body breathing. Let your breathing relax all of you.

Check the tension points. Press your eyes tightly for a few seconds, and release immediately and this will free your forehead of its intensity. Let your head tip forward in slow motion and the tension muscles of your neck will relax. Let your jaw loose and let it take a gentle yawn.

Begin to experience your whole body smiling. Feel how good it is to be here, now, and have nothing to do but *be*. Be aware of the mystery of your own breath. The Hebrews thought of their breath as the breath of God; it did not belong to them, it was His. His presence in them made them alive. When God took back His breath, death returned their body to earth. Be conscious that you breathe in the Spirit so that you can send forth the Word.

Now without moving your hands begin to become aware of the air at your fingertips, between your fingers, on the palms of your hands. It is always there, the delicate touch of the atmosphere and the gentle pressure of gravity. But we are not aware of this because all day our senses are drawing us out of ourselves and we rarely are this present to ourselves.

Become aware of the openness of your hands. This is the oldest gesture of prayer known to man, to man deeply conscious of the mystery of his own existence, his hands extended in offering and in reception, to give and to accept. When man is quiet and alone he is always close to wonder. He knows that he is in the Presence of Someone beyond himself, the world, and all others. The man of faith calls this Presence God, God who speaks to man and reveals Himself. God spoke to Moses and gave him His name — "I am who am and as who I am I will be with you." This promise became flesh in Christ who speaks His "I am" in us and calls us to echo His words in return, "I am with you," "We are with You."

Unless you become like little children, you cannot enter the kingdom." "The Kingdom of heaven is within you." Now go into your center where you are most yourself; to the room where you can pray to your Father in secret, "to the light which is at the still-point of the turning world," the inmost self of the psalms, the holy of holies where we meet Christ in Eucharist. Experience how good it is to be you and to hear yourself able to say "I am," "I am me," and, "It is good to be the me that I am."

Let the Word of God echo itself in you:

"In Him we live and move and have our being."

"Do you not know that you are the temple of God and that His Spirit lives in you?"

"If you but knew the gift of God and who it is that speaks to you."
"I will come to you and my Father will come to you and we will make our home in you."

"All things are yours, and you are Christ's and Christ is God."

"You are dead and your life is hidden with Christ in God."

"I live now, not I, but Christ lives in me."

Be at peace in the depths of your heart which He has created in His own image. There is a holy well within each of us. Let this well of peace and of love sink deeper. Remember the cumulative deposit of His presence in you through His Word, Sacrament and the people sent into your life.

Wait, be patient with God. Be like a faithful hound at the foot of his master, a beggar at the door of a cathedral, a fisherman before the ocean. The Spirit can touch in many ways, through our mind, imagination, memory, affectivity. He can influence the way we remember the past or anticipate the future. He can influence our desires, our convictions, our moving in one way or another.

Listen to Him call you by name, asking you the old, ever new question He asks of all His disciples:
"Whom do you say I am?"

"Do you love Me?"

"What do you want, for what are you searching?" (John, 1, 38).

"What do you want me to do for you?" Luke 18, 41).
"Do you believe me?" (John 11, 26).

He may come to us in an event of the Gospel, a mystery of the Rosary, a station of the Cross. To each of us Jesus gives a unique fragment of His Gospel which becomes a seed and core for our way of discipleship. There are certain words of power that call us as do no other words. It is the Holy Spirit who gives us the Christian "mantra." It is He who enables us to pray and to take the

Word from the level of thought down into the heart where it lives itself with every heart beat. A man can be transformed by one Word filled by the Spirit. "Father;" "Lord;" "Jesus;" Mercy; Peace; Light; Life; Truth; Glory; Holy; Come; Go.

When the time available is finished let us express our inner prayer of thanksgiving for what He has done in us. Let us become aware of our presence extending beyond our bodies, rippling out and interpenetrating the presence of the others with us in His presence. Let our presence and consciousness expand beyond the walls of the room into and across our city, state, nation, world, and know that in Him we are stretched to the fullness of His dimensions, of His consciousness and heart.

Then in slow motion open your eyes and continuing in the silence, write out of your stream of consciousness.

## OBJECT MEDITATION                      *Exercise in Sacramentality*

"Unless you become like little children
. . . ."

What is so lovely about little children is their sense of wonder and joyful imagination. They animate, personalize, companion everything in their lives. Too soon we grow old and "have eyes that do not see, ears that do not hear, and hands that cannot touch." To let our sense of wonder die is to close ourselves to the sacred and sacramental.

*Let us begin:*

Go outside and let some natural object choose you; a stone, a flower, blade of grass, weed, feather, grains of sand, pine cone, seashell, leaf, — anything which you can hold in your hand that exists in its natural state and is not processed or manufactured.

Take the same posture as in the exercise in adoration. Eyes closed, tune into your breathing, relax tension points, go into your deep center. Become aware of the air at your fingertips and now of the object resting in your hand. Without touching it with your fingers become aware of how it makes itself felt in your hand: the surface it covers; its weight; its warmth or coolness; its texture. Now reverently begin to explore your object with your fingers. How differently you come to know through touch. Realize how your eyes cannot see its firmness or softness; its flexibility or resistance: its roughness or smoothness. Be aware of how it changes through your touch, takes on your warmth, contracts or expands.

Now raise your object to your cheek, notice how different the touch of your cheek is from that of your hand.

Pass your object across your ear and listen to its sound. Now draw it close to your nose and detect its scent. Touch it to your lips and, if you wish, taste it with the tip of your tongue. Now lower your object gently and reverently to your lap.

Everything that is has a language, has something to say. Everything that is has value and meaning. Everything that is has a secret and is a mystery. Everything that is has a history, has come a long way. Everything that is is on a journey, has a destiny. Everything that is has something to share, something to give, something to say, something to receive. Everything that is has something to speak to you about yourself, to teach you something that nothing else could teach you.

Unless you become like a little child you will not understand, you will not receive the gift and wisdom that is waiting for you. So in your imagination become the size of your object, go into its center, learn its history, experience something of its destiny. Or let your object become your size and take it into your center. Give yourself to your object, be with it, go with it for a little while on its journey, listen to it, learn from it, discover its name . . . (15 minutes).

Now it is time to say goodbye to your friend. What makes it so important is the time you have wasted with it. Express your gratitude to it in some tangible way.

Now lift your object closer to your face so that as you open your eyes all that you will see is your new friend. . . . . When you wish, begin to write from your stream of consciousness.

This is the kind of prayer that fills the psalms. From the experiences of everyday things the mind and heart is lifted to Him from whom all things flow. Everything is a gift of God's love, goodness, wonder and beauty. Everything can be a sacrament of God, an epiphany, a transparency of His presence. There is nothing in creation or man's experience that has not been an occasion of man's recognizing the power and presence of God. Our Lord took bread and wine, water and oil, human word and gesture and made of them encounters with Himself.

The sacraments and psalms can teach us how to pray and how to discern His presence and love in all the things of our day. If we do not recognize Him, "the very stones will cry out." If we do not let our hearts grow hard as our arteries can, we will be prayed in constantly and like Him we will each day eternalize the lilies of the field and the birds of the air. What have you gathered into your heart? What are you bringing to His kingdom? So much waits for you; so much waits to be returned to Him in you.

*HAND*
*MEDITATION*

*Exercise in*
*Community*

Same posture as in other meditations —
eyes closed, hands resting in lap, palms
up, tune into your breathing, relax tension points and go into your center.

Become aware of the air at your fingertips,
between your fingers, on the palm of
your hand. Experience the fullness,
strength and maturity of your hands.
Think of your hands, think of the most
unforgettable hands you have known —
the hands of your father, your mother,
your grandparents. Remember the oldest
hands that have rested in your hands.
Think of the hands of a new born child,
your nephew or niece — of the incredible
beauty, perfection, delicacy in the hands
of a child. Once upon a time your hands
were the same size.

Think of all that your hands have done
since then. Almost all that you have
learned has been through your hands —
turning yourself over, crawling and creep-
ing, walking and balancing yourself; learning to hold something for the first time;
feeding yourself, washing and bathing,
dressing yourself. At one time your greatest accomplishment was tying your own
shoes.

Think of all the learning your hands have
done and how many activities they have

mastered, the things they have made. Remember the day you could write your own name.

Our hands were not just for ourselves but for others. How often they were given to help another. Remember all the kinds of work they have done, the tiredness and aching they have known, the cold and the heat, the soreness and the bruises. Remember the tears they have wiped away, our own or another's, the blood they have bled, the healing they have experienced. How much hurt, anger and even violence they have expressed, and how much gentleness, tenderness and love they have given.

How often they have been folded in prayer; both a sign of their powerlessness and of their power. Our father and mother guided these hands in the great symbolic language of our hands – the sign of the cross, the striking of our breast, the handshake, the wave of the hand in "hello" or "goodbye."

There is a mystery which we discover in the hand of a woman or the hand of a man that we love. There are the hands of a doctor, a nurse, an artist, a conductor, a priest, hands which you can never forget.

Now raise your right hand slowly and gently place it over your heart. Press more firmly until your hand picks up the beat of your heart, that most mysterious of all human sounds, one's own heartbeat, a rhythm learned in the womb from the heartbeat of one's mother. Press more firmly for a moment and then release your hand and hold it just a fraction from your clothing. Experience the warmth between your hand and your heart. Now lower your hand to your lap very carefully as if it were carrying your heart. For it does. When you extend your hand to another, it is not just bone and skin, it is your heart. A handshake is the real heart transplant.

Think of all the hands that have left their imprint on you. Fingerprints and handprints are heartprints that can never be erased. The hand has its own memory. Think of all the places that carry your handprints and all the people who bear your heartprint. They are indelible and will last forever.

Now without opening your eyes extend your hands on either side and find another hand. Do not simply hold it but explore it and sense the history and mystery of this hand. Let your hand speak to it and let it listen to the other. Try to express your gratitude for this hand stretched out to you in the dark and then bring your hand back again to your lap. Experience the presence of that hand lingering upon your hand. The afterglow will fade but the print is there forever.

Whose hand was that? It could have been any hand; it could have been His hand. It was. He has no other hands than ours.

Now begin to write out of your stream of consciousness.

*ABANDONMENT. Exercise in listening to one's own prayer.*

The prayers we say most frequently are the most difficult prayers to pray. There is no area of life where illusion is more dangerous and easy than in prayer. We can be *saying* prayers long after we have ceased praying. The psalms are not prayers in themselves; scripture is not prayer; reading is not prayer. The response in faith, hope and love is prayer, not the reading or saying.

*Let us begin:*

### PRAYER OF ABANDONMENT

Father,

I abandon myself into your hands;
do with me what you will.
Whatever you may do, I thank you:
I am ready for all, I accept all.
Let only your will be done in me,
and in all your creatures —
I wish no more than this, O Lord.

Into your hands I commend my soul;
I offer it to you with all the love of my
    heart,
for I love you Lord,
and so need to give myself,

to surrender myself into your hands,
without reserve,
and with boundless confidence,

For you are my Father.

Read this *Prayer Of Abandonment.* It is
Charles de Foucauld's personalized trans-
lation of the "Our Father." We do not
pray until the words of a prayer become
our own thought, feeling and action.
What part of this prayer do you find most
easy to pray? What is most difficult? I
find it easiest to say, "I most need to give
myself." I am finding it most difficult
to say, "I love you Lord." I can almost
hear Him exclaim, "You what!?"

I remember being on a panel with a Rabbi
and hearing him say with sadness, "We
have had two thousand years of Christian
'love.' Let's have no more of it." I have so
carelessly betrayed the word "love" that I
am afraid to say it.

The other expression I find difficult to
pray is "Father." I begin to realize how
little I let Him be Father to me. In my
arrogant and blind independence I know
that my life is far from being centered in
Him.

The greatest danger in each of us is the
distance between our eyes and our feet,
our vision and our behavior, our thoughts
and our activity. We can see the distant
mountain in a fraction of a moment but

it may take our whole life to climb it. We may know the answer to our problem but we can postpone acknowledging it for years. Even Foucauld could say, "My words are stronger than my heart."

Meditation on each of these thoughts and discernment of the reality, or lack thereof, supporting my words is the first stage in praying this prayer.

*Second Stage:*

Read and contemplate this prayer again but instead of addressing it to the Father, put in the names of the people with whom you live and work each day — John, Mary, Tom, Jane, etc. "I abandon myself into your hands . . . ." How does this affect your prayer? Is it possible to give yourself to another in this way? What do you find possible to say? What do you find most difficult?

What I find most difficult is, "Do with me what *you will.* Whatever you may do, *I thank you."* What is easiest is the last line, "For you are mine."

The terrifying test of our prayer is expressed in the Last Judgment, Matthew 25, "As long as you have not done this to the least of these my brothers, you have not done it to me." Jesus has identified himself with every man and, as with Paul, at any moment a light may come and we hear his voice, "I am Jesus and you are persecuting me."

How could we dare trust ourselves to another person so totally? How could we trust ourselves? Would it be good for them; would it be good for us? What would happen if we did? Would it be human, let alone Christian to do so? What would happen if someone entrusted himself totally to me? It is not altogether rare. Every friendship, every love moves in that direction. We forget the awesome creative power we have in each other's lives. When someone trusts us totally and completely, they compel us to grow, to measure up to their love, to become what they believe us to be. Each of us has incredible power to enable each other to grow and to become a new person in the measure we believe in them, hope in them and love them into a new fullness which they never recognized in themselves. We discover a new self-concept through the love and trust another has in us; we are born again. We are humbled, frightened by such love, such trust. We are more comfortable with our enemies and strangers who cannot ask from us. The more honest we are with ourselves, the more we realize that we do *not* pray like this; we *cannot* pray like this.

*Third Stage.*

Only Jesus can pray like this, only Jesus can say, "Father" with the fullest depth of his being. We cannot pray the PRAYER OF ABANDONMENT. This is Jesus' prayer alone. But if we desire,

Jesus will teach us and enable us to pray his prayer.

Now listen to Jesus pray this prayer to you. In place of the word "Father" and "Lord," put your own name and take time to try to listen to the way Jesus says your name, the way he calls you. He says your name as no one has ever said or will ever say your name. He calls you as only He who made you can call you, and he compels you to experience something of the fulness he has implanted in you because you are his image and likeness.

Listen to the depths of his word to you.

This is the prayer of your creation, of your being called into existence. This is the prayer of his baptism of you. This is the prayer of Eucharist which he prays and does each day in you. This is the prayer of Ordination, of Profession, of Marriage, of Discipleship. This is the prayer of the saints that renders Christ present in every generation in every situation of life.